UNDERSTANDING POLITICAL THEORY

THOMAS A. SPRAGENS, JR.

UNDERSTANDING POLITICAL THEORY

ST. MARTIN'S PRESS
New York

PREFACE

Those of us who study or teach political theory take its importance almost for granted. We know that the classic works of political theory embody the searching reflections of some very great minds on profound issues that confront every man and woman. We find it hard to imagine trying to make sense of our own political predicament without the aid of the conceptual touchstones found in the tradition of political thought.

We also appreciate the necessity of confronting the original sources of political theory firsthand. But the coherence and significance of political theorizing is not immediately apparent in any selection of the epic theories. Indeed, they may easily seem to be a rather motley collection of antiquarian esoterica— a largely random sample of essays, treatises, and dialogues composed by authors who speak different tongues.

The diligent student will eventually penetrate this surface variety and confusion and begin to understand what is going on. But it is not an easy task, and it has been made even more difficult by some of the more influential epistemological and metaphysical fashions of our day.

I have tried to make this sketch of political theory as a mode of inquiry intelligible to any literate person interested in the subject. My aim has been to be reasonably clear without being too simplistic or pedestrian, and to be somewhat original without being merely idiosyncratic.

The measure of my success will be the degree to which I can contribute to the understanding and appreciation of political theory. For understanding political theory is more than a worthwhile feat in its own right: it is a pathway toward the examined life for the individual and toward the reasoned public discourse that sustains a free society.

I would like to acknowledge the help of Isaac Kramnick, William T. Bluhm, and Max Skidmore, each of whom read the book in its original manuscript form. I have acted on almost all of their suggestions, thereby improving this essay in several ways. Since I chose, at my own peril, to ignore a few other of their suggestions, they can legitimately claim credit for some of the book's virtues without being responsible for any of its weaknesses.

I also want to thank Terry Brooks, Louise Walker, and Meri-Li Douglas for their invaluable work in preparing the manuscript. I'm not sure what I, or my Duke colleagues, would do without their assistance.

THOMAS A. SPRAGENS, JR.

CONTENTS

UNDERSTANDING
POLITICAL
THEORY

ONE

POLITICS AND POLITICAL THEORY: AN INTRODUCTION

"Political theory" is a term with several meanings. The discipline of political science is today a house with many mansions, and each of these mansions, or subfields of political science, is concerned with theory in one form or another.

The type of political theory which this book examines is called by some "normative" political theory, by others "political philosophy." To borrow a phrase from Professor Sheldon Wolin, we might also call it "epic" theory.[1]

Whatever the term that seems most useful to characterize it, the form of political theory which is our concern here is the form of inquiry embodied in acknowledged classics such as Plato's *Republic*, the *Leviathan* of Thomas Hobbes, and Rousseau's *Social Contract*. These works attempt to provide a profound and relatively comprehensive vision of political life. *Theōrein*, the Greek word from which we get our word "theory," meant "to look at, to behold, to contemplate." That is what these great thinkers, and others like them who have engaged in the centuries-old dialogue of political theory, enable us to do. They provide us with a way of looking at politics which adds up to "a symbolic picture of an ordered whole."[2] They give us a "vision," a full-scale way of understanding the world of politics in which we must live.

1

The Ends and Means of Politics

Much of contemporary political science is concerned with power and influence. Seeking to answer the question "Who governs?" it focuses on the decision-making process in society, trying to understand how political decisions are made and who makes them. It is concerned, in David Easton's phrase, with the "authoritative allocation of values" in society. To use Harold Lasswell's very blunt language, it considers the study of politics to be the study of "who gets what, when, how."

The study of the decision-making process is both fascinating and important. No one can claim to understand a political society unless he has a rather good grasp of the mechanisms, processes, and persons or groups which determine the policy "outputs" of that society. The sociology of power, therefore, is a crucial part of the study of politics.

There is much more to politics than the struggle for power, however. At least there is much more to politics than the struggle for power if the society in question is to be more than the "war of all against all." A political society is also a framework of ordered relationships within which we are enabled to live together and to satisfy our communal wants and needs. A political society, in short, is a meaningful human *enterprise*. It is not merely an event, something that happens. It is an intentional human creation, devised and directed to accomplish important practical goals.

The ends of politics are generated by the necessities of human life. Even physical survival in this world requires organized effort. And the creation of a form of life which is more than mere survival involves the creation of more and more sophisticated "political" institutions. Human beings need security—protection from the onslaught of nature and from the aggression of other men. They need food, shelter, and clothing. They also need, though perhaps less immediately, means for the expression of their more distinctively human qualities—ways of achieving identity and companionship, for example.

None of these human needs are satisfied simply by wishing it so. We don't live in a Garden of Eden where all our desires are met by nature. We can survive and prosper only by our own human effort—by *work*. We must create and build with our own minds and hands the institutions which enable us to become "civilized."

The purposes, or "functions," of political society are therefore numerous and varied. At the most basic level, the social order must furnish its members with protection. It has to guarantee their physical security. And it has to provide some kind of guarantee that the fruits of its members' labor will be secure, as well. Even the most limited conception of the purposes of political society include this much—the protection of what John Locke termed "life, liberty, and estate." In most human societies, moreover, the economic productive process—the creation of goods and services—requires an organized communal effort. Institutions must be established, therefore, for the production and distribution of wealth. The creation and regulation of such institutional arrangements are also important functions of politics. As political theorists from Aristotle to Marx have observed, these arrangements are absolutely central to the life and governance of any political system.

At a still more sophisticated level, a political society provides a framework of meaning and significance for its members. It brings some human order out of chaos. It is a kind of drama—a play which provides roles for its citizens. And people fashion their identities out of these roles. In the words of a contemporary political theorist, a political society is "a little world, a *cosmion*, illuminated with meaning from within by the human beings who continuously create and bear it as the mode and condition of their self-realization."[3]

Political societies articulate and celebrate their meaning—their overarching purposes—through rituals of all kinds. By singing national anthems, pledging allegiance to the flag, and honoring their founding fathers, the members of a society participate in and express their support of the larger meanings which their society seeks to embody. In some societies all of this is especially evident: the schools, the newspapers, the arts all seek to inculcate an understanding of the purposes of the society. In totalitarian regimes, these efforts are integrated and censored so that they speak with one voice. But even pluralistic societies celebrate the meaning of their politics with enthusiasm—not only in official ways, but with spontaneous patriotic hoopla such as the halftime show at the Orange Bowl.

The Purposes and Relevance of Political Theory

Like all enterprises directed toward established goals, political societies may be successes or they may be failures. They may achieve their ends or they may fall woefully short. A political society may contribute immeasurably to the lives of its citizens, giving them security, prosperity, justice, and a sense of dignity. Or, by failing in its appointed tasks, a political society can be a curse, bringing its members misery, bloodshed, oppression, and a sense of futility.

The goal of political theory, as we stated at the outset, is to provide a "comprehensive vision" of the political enterprise. A political theorist tries to give his audience the "big picture" by putting politics into full perspective. Specifically, he tries to understand politics by looking at it against the background of human nature and other features of our world which we must take as "givens."

A comprehensive vision of this sort is both descriptive and evaluative. Descriptively, a political theory identifies the most important actors, forces, and structures that make up political life; and it explains the basic relationships that obtain among these variables which it has identified. Marxist theory, for example, points out to us the economic forces and social class patterns that it sees at the heart of the political process. Enlightenment liberals identify and explain the scientific and intellectual forces which they see as the engine of human progress. Thomas Hobbes, Plato, and Aristotle (among others) all provide extensive and profound analyses of the political impact of human passions and ambitions. Jeremy Bentham and James Madison explore and interpret the role that legislation and constitutional mechanisms play in the outcomes of politics. And so on. The core of any political theory is a broad descriptive account of what is going on beneath the surface sound and fury of human politics.[4]

Comprehensive descriptions of human activity such as these, by virtue of their breadth and profundity, have an important evaluative dimension as well. The political landscapes depicted in political theories are not empty vistas of neutral data. They are instead depictions of order and chaos, of triumph and tragedy, of sublime achievement and dismal failure, of community and warfare, of progress and disintegration. By enabling us to see the totality of politics, the political theorist enables us to see what is destructive or inadequate or foolish or irrational about some of our own political institutions and actions. Aristotle, for example, points out how constitutions that are not adapted to the culture of a given society are likely to fail; Plato explains the political dangers of undisciplined passions; Hobbes shows us the folly of pursuing our short-run desires without heed for the ultimate disasters they may produce; Marx illuminates the irrationality of "commodity fetishism"; Madison explains the imprudence of vesting all powers of government in the same hands. A political theory provides a basis for judging the wisdom of our political deeds and arrangements by looking at them in the full context of the human needs and limitations that created politics in the first place. We are provided with perspective on what we are doing and thereby given some grounds for seeing how well we are doing it.

Clearly, then, political theory is not merely of "academic" interest. It is, to borrow an overworked adjective, highly "relevant" to the practical political issues that confront us every day. While the theorist writes in part simply to satisfy his own intellectual passions—to comprehend the world in which he must live—he also writes for the practical benefit of his audience. Almost all political theorists manifestly believe that we would be better off it we heeded their message—if we would, as Hobbes wrote, "convert this truth of speculation into the utility of practice."[5] A political theory, then, tries to make the world of politics intelligible to us in order to provide us with guidance. It sketches for us the geography of politics; and this kind of map tells us where we stand and what routes will take us where we need to go.

Some political theorists have believed that, by paying heed

to their insights, we might overcome the conflicts and frustrations of life in society and create a fully harmonious and satisfying political order. Others, less optimistic, have at least hoped that their understanding of politics might help to prevent or to mitigate potential political disasters. Even Hobbes, whose vision of politics was on the whole very bleak, felt that he could help us to avoid lives that were "solitary, poor, nasty, brutish, and short."

The fact that political theories offer visions of politics, symbolic pictures of an ordered whole, is reflected in the metaphors of sight which appear at crucial places in classic theories. Moreover, these metaphors of sight are often phrased so as to express the practical importance of the view being offered. The political theories are intended to remedy defects in the way that most of us see politics—defects that may carry calamitous consequences. Where there is no vision, the psalmist tells us, the people perish. Most great political theories could take that admonition as their motto.

Men may, for example, fall into political disasters from their extreme *shortsightedness*. Preoccupied by their immediate concerns and desires, they may fail to look ahead until it is too late. Intent upon seeking personal fame or fortune, they may allow a situation to develop in which they lose all they had struggled to get and more. By pursuing their individual wants, heedless of the ultimate consequences of their acts, men may stumble into civil wars, riots, destructive political turmoil. Corrected vision, enabling men to take a broader view, might prevent these disasters. At least this is what Thomas Hobbes, whose *Leviathan* has been called the greatest "masterpiece of political philosophy written in the English language,"[6] hoped to accomplish with his political theory—which he called "moral or civil science." "All men," he wrote, "are by nature provided of notable multiplying glasses, (that is their passions and self-love,) through which every little payment appeareth a great grievance; but are destitute of those prospective glasses, (namely moral and civil science) to see a far off the miseries that hang over them, and cannot without such payments be avoided."[7]

Plato, in his *Republic*, which was the first great work of

Western political theory, also resorted continually to metaphors of sight to explain his purposes. The "visual" defects which he perceived are different ones from the shortsightedness that Hobbes found to be at the bottom of man's political predicament. Right in the middle of his dialogue, Plato fashioned his justly famous "allegory of the cave" to explain the problem. Most of us, he said, are like people who have lived all their lives in a cave. All we have seen are the shadows and images that flicker on the cave walls. Having never seen the light of day, we do not even know that what we see are only shadows. Without capacity to see how things really are, then, we create and live within a political world of illusions. And, because a belief in illusions can be as dangerous as extreme shortsightedness, we stumble blindly into political disorders that may destroy the soul as well as the body.

The remedy for this kind of visual defect is not as simple as providing lenses to correct shortsightedness. In Plato's view, men must be enabled not simply to see further, but to see differently. They need not lenses, but light. Providing men with spectacles won't do the job. They need to be re-oriented, turned around altogether in their vision of the world. For Hobbes, political theory could achieve its goals by providing foresight. For Plato, the vision of political theory must bring a kind of conversion. "Just as one might have to turn the whole body round in order that the eye should see light instead of darkness," he wrote, "so the entire soul must be turned away from this changing world, until its eye can bear to contemplate reality and that supreme splendour which we have called the Good."[8]

More recently, to take another example, Herbert Marcuse has argued that prevailing modes of discourse and of political organization have limited and distorted our vision of politics. They have created a pervasive form of "false consciousness." "To the degree to which they correspond to the given reality," he wrote in One-Dimensional Man, "thought and behavior express a false consciousness, responding to and contributing to the preservation of a false order of facts. And this false consciousness has become embodied in the prevailing technical apparatus which in turn reproduces it."[9] This failure of vision, this

false consciousness, has in his view profound political consequences. It robs us of our freedom. It prevents us from realizing
the possibilities for human fulfillment made possible by ad-
vanced industrial society. The task, the hope, the promise of
political theory is to deliver us from this failure of vision and
therefore from the "repressiveness" of our social arrangements.
The critical vision of reason, of political *theōria*, "is the subversive power" [10] that enables humanity to become truly liberated.

When they get down to specifics, political theorists such as
Hobbes, Plato, and Marcuse obviously disagree on many, many
things. They disagree very profoundly, in fact. The voices of
political theorists make up a dialogue, a conversation, not a
chorus. But political theorists share some fundamental under-
standings about their form of inquiry that enable them to speak
to one another across vast reaches of time, space, and political
culture. It is not easy, they would insist, to "see" what the world
of politics is all about. Indeed, our vision is generally quite
limited and often positively distorted. These failures to comprehend politics, to see it in its totality, can be dangerous and
destructive. It is therefore important to overcome the defects of
political perception as best we can. That necessity constitutes
the task of political theory.

Ways of Understanding Political Theory

There are several ways, all of them useful, to characterize
and define a field of inquiry. It is possible, for example, to
answer the question "What is political theory?" by looking at
its *problems*. Or we might wish to look at its *goals*. Or, again,
we might look instead at its *propositions*.

If we try to define political theory by its problems, we can
identify certain issues that seem to reverberate throughout its
tradition. These "perennial questions" reappear with a persis-
tence which clearly marks them as central to the concern of
political theory. "Are there natural standards of justice?"
"What is the proper relationship between the individual and the
community?" "Who should be entrusted with power?" "In what
ways can the state contribute to human freedom, and in what

ways must it constrain human freedom?" These questions, and others like them, confront men whenever they face up to the task of constructing or reforming or rebelling against a political society. These questions, therefore, in one form or another, concern almost all political theorists and, directly or indirectly, they must be faced. Recognition and appreciation of the perennial issues of political theory, then, can take us a long way toward an understanding of the enterprise.[11]

It is also possible to try to grasp the nature of political theory by analyzing its purposes, its goals. What are political theorists looking for? What do they want to know? Those who take this approach usually conclude that political theory is an inquiry into what makes the "good society." Leo Strauss, one of the most eminent authorities in political theory, for example, has said that political philosophy is "an attempt truly to know both the nature of political things and the right, or the good, political order."[12] His definition is helpful. Certainly all of the great political theorists have shared this common concern—to know and to articulate what makes a political society a good one, one which human beings will find satisfying, one which will not leave them insecure or miserable.

Finally, we might try to define political theory by its formal products. What kinds of claims does it make? What sorts of propositions does it generate? Because political theories generally contain implications and recommendations for action, this approach usually characterizes the tradition of political theory as "normative" theory: that is, political theory is a form of inquiry which makes prescriptions and sets standards. Normative theory tries to tell us what we ought to do or should do. It makes claims about obligations, duties, and ideals.

Each of these approaches, singly or in combination, offers valuable insight into the nature of political theory. Indeed, it would be impossible to understand any intellectual enterprise without having some clear apprehension of the basic problems which it confronts, the intellectual ends it seeks to attain, and the kinds of propositions which come from it.

Nevertheless, these accounts, essential as they are, remain partial and incomplete. For one thing, although they tell us something about the beginning and the ends of political theory, the types of questions it addresses and the kinds of answers that it gives, these accounts tell us very little about the *middle,* and how we get from one point to another. To fill in the picture, we need to know not only what some of the crucial questions are, but how theorists have gone about trying to answer them; not only what the goals are, but how political theorists have tried to reach them; and not only what sorts of propositions are produced by political theorists, but where they come from and how they are justified.

"Logic-in-use" vs. "Reconstructed Logic"

If we are really to understand what goes on in any form of inquiry, I am suggesting, we have to look very closely at its intellectual *processes.* We have to attend to what Professor Abraham Kaplan has called the "logic-in-use" of the enterprise.[13]

As Professor Kaplan observes, the "logic" of a discipline that we can reproduce, or reconstruct, by piecing together its propositional structure ex post facto is one thing; the actual cognitive procedures or logic-in-use is something else. These procedures, moreover, are not identical with the "reconstructed logic," nor can they be *reduced* to it. While logic-in-use and reconstructed logic obviously overlap, "we can no more take them to be identical or even assume an exact correspondence between them, than we can in the case of the decline of Rome and Gibbon's account of it, a patient's fever and his physician's explanation of it."[14]

There is reason to believe, moreover, that preoccupation with the reconstructed logic of a mode of inquiry, in isolation from its dynamic logic-in-use, may produce a misleading and distorted account of the matter. Reconstructed logics are idealizations. They are also abstractions. And any idealized abstraction, whatever its virtues, is an embryonic misconception.

If we rely exclusively, or even primarily, upon ex post facto reconstructions of a given form of inquiry as a basis for understanding what it is all about, therefore, we may come up short. In fact, we may be positively misled. Thomas Kuhn, for one, has argued in his essay *The Structure of Scientific Revolutions* that this is exactly what has happened in the realm of natural science. By drawing our image of science, "from the study of finished scientific achievements," he writes, "we have been misled . . . in fundamental ways."[15]

Whatever the case in natural science, it is certain that political theories are not satisfactorily comprehended by looking at them as sets of propositions. We can learn a great deal from this approach, but we also will miss a lot. And a lot of what we miss is important. Political theories, we have said, are symbolic pictures of ordered wholes. They are ways of seeing the world. When a theorist tries to communicate his vision of the political world, when he tries to get us to "see things his way," he will use a very mixed bag of strategies and syntactical forms. Besides simple declarative statements, he will probably have to use significant analogies, metaphors and similes, maxims, imaginative stories and myths, exhortations and imperatives. He can't simply use the same old words in an unproblematic way. For these words take their meaning from the "language-games" within which they function (as the eminent twentieth-century philosopher Ludwig Wittgenstein has so ably shown us); and the political theorist is trying to make us understand a whole new ball game.

Moreover, abstract logic dictates the separation of "is" and "ought." In strictly logical terms, no series of statements about what *is* the case can dictate what *should* be done. Yet the hallmark of political theory is the way in which these two concepts are brought together, if not "logically" at least "naturally." Reconstructed logic, then, requires us to separate out the "descriptive" from the "prescriptive" components of political theories; and once again the results are distorting. The requirements of static ex post facto logic seem to compel us to miss one of the central features of political theory. Within its limitations we cannot understand the way in which a particular way of seeing the world generates a set of responses which seem to be normal and proper. We are blocked from appreciating the crucial way in which a broad vision of political reality "secretes a notion of good, and a set of valuations, which cannot be done away with."[16]

The reconstructed-logic approach also manages to suppress and obscure the whole existential dimension of political theory which makes it so alive and fascinating. In the real world, political theory deals in starkly human problems. It begins with predicaments, dilemmas, frustrations, and crises which it tries desperately to resolve or overcome. It is all bound up with human wants and needs, striving intensely to promote their satisfaction. To begin a study of political theory through its reconstructed logic, then, is not really wrong or useless, but it's rather like beginning to study human life by studying cadavers.

Because the ex post facto abstractions of reconstructed logic can be misleading, the starting point for understanding a mode of inquiry, such as political theory, should not be the propositions which it generates. Instead, the starting point must be, in the words of philosopher of science Stephen Toulmin, "the living, historically-developing intellectual enterprise within which concepts find their collective use." As Toulmin suggests, "This change of approach obliges us to abandon all those static, 'snapshot' analyses in which philosophers have for so long discussed the concepts current in the natural sciences and other intellectual activities. Instead, we must give a more historical, 'moving picture' account of our intellectual enterprises and procedures, in which we can finally hope to understand the historical dynamics of conceptual change, and so recognize the nature and sources of its 'rationality.'"[17]

Reading the Classics

The classics of political theory provide much of this concrete historical record which is so essential. Retracing the steps of acknowledged masters, we learn by apprenticeship. If we are able to understand the concrete concerns, aims, and perceptions of a Rousseau or a Locke or a Hegel, we have already surmounted some of the limitations of the "static snapshot" approach. In fact, scientists and scholars of all varieties learn their trade in precisely this way. They learn what it means to be a physicist, or a botanist, or a political theorist by following the example of established practitioners—not by reading some abstract handbook of methods.

Nevertheless, learning political theory *solely* by reading the classics, important as they are, also has its dangers and limitations.

In the first place, the classics themselves are "finished products," even though they don't take the form of systematic sets of propositions. They already embody a logic of *exposition*, which is rarely the same as the logic of the *inquiry* itself. By reading the *Social Contract* and the *Republic* attentively, we may achieve a fairly good comprehension of Rousseau's and Plato's visions of political order. But without a great deal of intellectual detective work it may well continue to be quite unclear to us where these finished visions came from, what caused Rousseau and Plato to see things the way they did, and why they found their views so compelling. We still may not comprehend their logic-in-use, in other words. And because of this failure, our understanding remains in some sense deficient.

Second, an exclusive reliance upon the study of finished classics may lead one to see political theories as museum pieces. The classics are products of past times and places. One might be led to assume, therefore, that political theory is merely a subcategory of intellectual history. And if that is what political theory is all about, then it is best left to intellectual historians or to those with an antiquarian curiosity. Professor David Easton has, in fact, argued that this train of thought is one of the principal causes of a recent decline in the significance accorded to political theory.[18]

Third, because they *are* the product of times and places which may be very different from our own, and because they may be expressed in patterns of discourse quite alien to our own, the classics may not be very intelligible—especially to a relative novice who has only a slight background in intellectual history. For example, Plato begins the *Republic* with a stroll down to the Piraeus, Hobbes begins his *Leviathan* with a consideration of the nature of motion, and Burke opens his *Reflections on the Revolution in France* with a polemic against Doctor Richard Price, "a non-conforming minister of eminence."

All of these starting points actually make very good sense—in dramatic, logical, and historical context respectively. But the sense they make is far from immediately apparent. The same holds true for frequently encountered apparent esoterica such as arguments about the "state of nature."

And, finally, because the classic works of political theory do assume such diverse forms and do speak in such diverse tongues, it may not be at all obvious that they comprise a reasonably coherent tradition of discourse and deal with largely the same problems. What these works have in common may easily not be clear. And if the common elements and concerns are not perceived, then it becomes difficult if not impossible to treat the theorists comparatively—to see how they speak to one another and to us across the barriers of time, place, and "language" (in the most profound sense of that word).

Yet, as all students of political theory well appreciate, the classics of political theory and the form of inquiry they embody in their different ways are neither unintelligible, nor are they of purely antiquarian interest, nor are they so diverse as to be noncomparable. Those who have invested the time and effort to crack the code, as it were, are well aware that the discussions and concerns of political theory are profoundly meaningful and perennially relevant. Indeed, all of us who inhabit and who make choices within a civil society are, to some extent, political theorists. We cannot help having, and acting upon, certain fundamental beliefs and perceptions about the nature of politics, even if those beliefs are in most cases rather inarticulate, poorly informed, and semicoherent.[19]

The purpose of political theory is to make the beliefs which guide our political actions explicit, coherent, and well-grounded. In this sense, the enterprise of political theory is one of the most profound expressions of man's quest to be a truly "rational" being, to be a creature led by the light of mind rather than merely an animal impelled by blind impulse. Political theorists are not distinctive by simply *having* political views; they are distinctive by the *quality* of these views. They are men and women who have tried to "make sense" of politics in a very fundamental way. They have sought to make their vision of politics explicit, coherent, and well-grounded in the best knowledge available about the nature of man and his world. All of us who share the goal of acting rationally can learn from them and profit by their example. Masters of political theory not only give us insight into the world of politics; they also show us what we must, to some extent, do for ourselves.

Political Theory: A Dynamic Framework

The chapters which follow are written to provide a framework for understanding political theory as a form of inquiry. Despite notable differences in style and in terminology, political theorists are not only concerned with the same basic problems; their attempts to solve these problems also tend to follow a fairly consistent pattern. This consistent pattern of inquiry is usually not explicit in the finished statements of the theorists. The order of exposition often reverses, and therefore obscures, the order of actual thought and discovery. The *conclusions* of the process of inquiry often emerge as the *premises* or opening theses of the exposition. But the pattern is there, nonetheless, if we are willing to look for it.

Following the lead of writers such as Toulmin, Kaplan, and Kuhn, the order of our own exposition seeks to follow the logic-in-use of political theory. We shall begin where the theorists themselves begin—not with conclusions, and not even with abstract questions, but rather with the concrete sense of puzzlement or concern which stimulates the inquiry in the first place. Once begun, the process begins to take on a certain dynamic of its own. The answer or solution to the initial problem poses another question, which then must be confronted in turn. The answer to that question poses another level of problems, and so on, until the theorist finally is driven to articulate his "symbolic vision of an ordered whole." At that point, and only at that point, can the theorist's intellectual explorations stop; for only an achievement of this sort can satisfy the concern which provided the initial impetus to his inquiry.

Our framework of the dynamic logic-in-use of political theory is neither very elaborate in its essentials nor (in basic outline, at least) peculiar to political theory alone. Instead, it is a model of a problem-solving intellect at work.

For problem solving is what political theorists are trying to do. "Problems" in political life, of course, are not merely intellectual puzzles. They are genuine *predicaments*. And this is where the political theorist begins—with the political predicament of his society. He wants to understand its nature and dimensions, with an eye toward enabling people to cope with it—not wholly on a trial and error basis, but with some more thought-out strategy based on a deeper grasp of the issues at hand.

Our consideration of the logic-in-use of political theory will therefore begin, in chapter 2, with the theorist's dawning recognition of the human political predicament.

Almost all political theories seem to originate from a perception of disorder in the body politic. Occasionally a political theorist comes along who is wholly at home with the status quo of his society and who is inspired by a purely intellectual curiosity to explore the foundations of that existing order. He is the exception rather than the rule. Most political theorists begin their work out of a growing sense that something is wrong in their society. Their first concern, therefore, becomes to identify the problem. Sometimes this is easy enough. The crisis of economic collapse or civil war may be evident to almost anyone. At other times, however, merely identifying the problem may call for some careful thought.

After identifying the problem to his own satisfaction, the theorist cannot stop there. He then must inquire into the sources of the difficulty. He must engage in a careful diagnosis of the political malfunction he has perceived. Discovering the causal forces at work behind a given problem is usually a very difficult and tricky task. Some of the more striking intellectual models of political theorists, therefore, have been devised in the attempt to accomplish this goal. We shall look at the process of diagnosis in chapter 3.

Next the theorist is naturally moved to consider what the political world would look like if the problem or predicament were dealt with as effectively as possible. Usually, he must use his imagination here. He is trying to envision the shape of a political order which does not at present exist. The theorist's imaginative reconstruction of the world of politics will be our concern in chapter 4.

Finally comes the component of political theory which is sometimes depicted as its distinctive characteristic—namely, the element of prescription. Having found failures in the functioning of the political system, having discovered some of the causes of this breakdown, and having articulated a vision of a regenerate political order, the theorist will very likely make some programmatic suggestions. He will naturally be inclined to offer recommendations for political action which would, in his view, best remedy the problems he has analyzed. Sometimes the theorist is very explicit and direct in his recommendations, like Machiavelli, whose maxims for rulers were the main focus of his writings. At other times these recommendations may be much less direct and systematic. In either case, what needs emphasis is the way these prescriptions are grounded in the preceding analysis. Chapter 5 will deal with this part of political theory.

In practice, the sequential order of these component steps may vary somewhat, but only within certain limits. Any prescriptive recommendations, for example, come at the end. Suggestions for concrete political action become rational and meaningful only after it has been made clear what the problem is, what its causes are, and what would constitute a viable alternative. Unless these prior foundations have been established, the prescriptions hang in a vacuum.

Similarly, the diagnostic analysis cannot logically precede the perception of disorder. The problem has to be clearly identified before one can proceed to investigate its causes.

Therefore 1) perception of disorder, 2) diagnosis, and 3) prescription always appear in that sequential order in the process of inquiry, whatever order they assume in the exposition of the theory.

The fourth component in the theoretical process, the imaginative reconstruction, is something of a "floater." It must precede the prescriptive recommendations, but it may either precede or follow the diagnosis; and it may even precede the full perception of disorder. In most cases, this reconstructed vision of politics seems to grow in stages, in a kind of dialectical interaction with the perception of disorder and the diagnosis.

The various steps of the process are closely interrelated, but they do not form a monolithic whole. The shape and content of each step of the inquiry define and limit the shape and content of the later steps very profoundly, without wholly determining them. Each successive stage in the process of inquiry builds upon the earlier ones; but each step also involves a creative addition which is more than a simple inference from what has come before.

For example, the diagnosis provided by a theorist clearly grows in part from the perception of disorder, since the perception of disorder identified the symptoms whose causes are in question. However, the outcome of the diagnostic process is not foreclosed at the outset, because merely specifying a symptomatic problem does not tell you its sources. Similarly, the recommendations offered by a theorist can be compelling only against the background of the analysis which precedes it. However, all sorts of new probability judgments and strategic decisions must also be made in reaching any final prescriptions.

One may, to take a specific case, fully agree with Plato that something must have been wrong with Athens if it could put Socrates to death, without agreeing with him that a society like the one he outlines in *The Republic* would be the best solution. Or one may very well be convinced by Karl Marx that a capitalist economy exploits and alienates the working class without advocating (or, more precisely in this case, without insisting upon the necessity of) a dictatorship of the proletariat.

NOTES

[1]Sheldon S. Wolin, "Political Theory as a Vocation," *American Political Science Review*, 62 (December 1969): pp. 1062-82.

[2]Ibid., p. 1080.

[3]Eric Voegelin, *The New Science of Politics* (Chicago: University of Chicago Press, 1952), p. 27.

[4]For an excellent discussion of this aspect of political theory, see William T.

Bluhm, *Theories of the Political System* (Englewood Cliffs, N.J.: Prentice-Hall, 1965).

[5] Thomas Hobbes, *Leviathan* (New York: E. P. Dutton, 1950), p. 319.

[6] Michael Oakeshott, "Introduction" to the *Leviathan* (Oxford: Basil Blackwell, 1974), p. viii.

[7] Thomas Hobbes, *Leviathan*, p. 154.

[8] Plato, *Republic*, VII, 518 (Cornford translation).

[9] Herbert Marcuse, *One-Dimensional Man* (Boston: Beacon Press, 1964), p. 145.

[10] Ibid., p. 123.

[11] For an introduction to political theory which takes this approach, see Glenn Tinder, *Political Thinking: The Perennial Questions*, 2nd ed. (Boston: Little, Brown, 1974).

[12] Leo Strauss, *What is Political Philosophy?* (New York: Free Press, 1959), p. 12.

[13] Abraham Kaplan, *The Conduct of Inquiry* (San Francisco: Chandler, 1964).

[14] Ibid., p. 8.

[15] Thomas S. Kuhn, *The Structure of Scientific Revolutions*, 2nd ed. (Chicago: University of Chicago Press, 1970), p. 1.

[16] Charles Taylor, "Neutrality in Political Science," in Laslett and Runciman, eds., *Philosophy, Politics, and Society*, 3rd series (New York: Barnes & Noble, 1967), p. 56.

[17] Stephen Toulmin, *Human Understanding* (Princeton, N.J.: Princeton University Press, 1972), vol. 1, p. 85.

[18] David Easton, *The Political System*, 2nd ed. (New York: Knopf, 1971), chapter 10.

[19] For an interesting study based upon this recognition of what he calls "latent ideology," see Robert E. Lane, *Political Ideology* (New York: Free Press, 1962).

TWO

CRISIS AND THE PERCEPTION OF DISORDER

Political theories are like pearls: they are not produced without an irritant. Most political theories, at least most of the "epic" theories, are written as attempts to deal with some very real and urgent problems. These problems *demand* the attention of the theorist; they don't merely invite inquiry. The theorist writes out of compelling practical necessity—the need to understand a political situation that is causing real trouble and real pain to those caught within it.

When people are happy, when they have little cause to complain about the state of their society, profound political theories are a rarity. Indeed, Edmund Burke claimed that an avid concern for political theory was a sign of a poorly run society. "The bulk of mankind," he wrote, "are not excessively curious concerning any theories whilst they are really happy; and one symptom of an ill-conducted state is the propensity of the people to resort to them."[1]

Americans, traditionally, have not been terribly concerned with political theory, presumably for some of the above reasons. Not that the United States has not seen its share of political conflict and turmoil. On the contrary. But the many group conflicts and confrontations in this society have tended to be conflicts of interest more than fights over basic principles. Our political battles have usually taken place within a larger, if not very well defined, agreement on fundamentals. For various historical and sociological reasons, Lockean liberal assumptions about political order have largely been taken for granted here. These assumptions have been taken for granted, in fact, to the point that they are rarely recognized for what they are. As Louis Hartz has written: "There has never been a 'liberal movement' or a real 'liberal party' in America: we have only had the American Way of Life, a nationalist articulation of Locke which usually does not know that Locke himself is involved."[2]

Relatively secure in their acceptance of often unarticulated and unrecognized fundamental beliefs about politics, Americans have tended to approach politics "pragmatically." If the basic foundations of the system are sound, or believed to be sound, then specific problems can be handled one at a time on a kind of trial-and-error basis. Instead of trying to look at the roots of political problems, where political theorizing would be relevant, we tend instead to "muddle through."

This lack of a propensity to resort to theories probably indicates a fairly stable political situation, in Burke's terms. However, this political plus is something of an intellectual minus. The lack of theoretical sophistication about politics exhibited by Americans may say something good about their political situation, but it is not anything to be proud of intellectually.

There are times, moreover, when the American obliviousness to political theory has its practical costs. It is one of the reasons, for example, behind some of the problems which the United States has in understanding and dealing with other nations. We often assume that everyone takes certain political principles for granted, just because we do. Our understanding of world conflicts, and hence our response to them, may suffer from this faulty assumption. Too often we are like the senator who wondered why the Arabs and the Israelis couldn't sit down and discuss their problems as good Christian gentlemen would do.

Even in domestic politics, a lack of theoretical sophistication may be a drawback. There are times when political problems run very deep, and we may not be able to deal with them satisfactorily simply by "muddling through." We may just muddle on into deeper trouble, unappreciative of the sources of our problems.

Socialization and "Subversion"

The profound and searching analysis of political order found in political theory not only seems practically rather pointless if everything is going well; it is also rather difficult. In every society, social mechanisms are always at work to encourage its members to accept and to internalize the established view of things. Children learn very early what the "proper" political attitudes and responses are. In this country, for example, we are taught very quickly that the American Way of Life is a good thing that we should all appreciate. We learn that "freedom" and "democracy" are great, and that our system is the foremost embodiment of these virtues. In other political systems the message is different, but the processes are similar. A Cuban child learns very early that "Yankee imperialism" is a great threat to his society and that Premier Fidel is the great leader who liberated his country.

These "truths" about the world of politics are absorbed in part from formal teachings and activities—civics classes and saluting the flag, as two examples—and in part from the more informal lessons we learn from the attitudes of those around us. If everyone around us seems fearful and anxious when "communism" or "fascism" or "Yankee imperialism" is mentioned, then we assume these phenomena must be dangerous. If everyone around us seems intensely respectful and devoted to the Constitution or to the "Founding Fathers" or to the "socialist fatherland," then we conclude that these must be fine things, worthy of our own loyalty.

In *Killers of the Dream*, Lillian Smith has given us a brilliant and sensitive account of the process of socialization in her own Southern childhood. She describes very well the way that beliefs about "correct" political and social behavior are communicated to the members, especially the young members, of any society:

> We were given no formal instruction in these difficult matters but we learned our lessons well. We learned the intricate system of taboos, of renunciations and compensations, of manners, voice modulations, words, feelings, along with our prayers, our toilet

habits, and our games. I do not remember how or when, but by the time I had learned that God is love, that Jesus is His Son and came to give us more abundant life, that all men are brothers with a common Father, I also knew that I was better than a Negro, that all black folks have their place and must be kept in it, that sex has its place and must be kept in it, that a terrifying disaster would befall the South if ever I treated a Negro as my social equal and as terrifying disaster would befall my family if ever I were to have a baby outside of marriage. . . .

From the day I was born, I began to learn my lessons. I was put in a rigid frame too intricate, too twisting to describe here so briefly, but I learned to conform to its slide-rule measurements. I learned it is possible to be a Christian and a white southerner simultaneously; to be a gentlewoman and an arrogant callous creature in the same moment; to pray at night and ride a Jim Crow car the next morning and to feel comfortable in doing both. I learned to believe in freedom, to glow when the word "democracy" was used, and to practice slavery from morning to night. . . .

And we learned far more from acts than words, more from a raised eyebrow, a joke, a shocked voice, a withdrawing movement of the body, a long silence, than from long sentences.[3]

The internalization of these lessons about the geography of the political world go very deep. They rarely reach the surface. It seems neither necessary nor wholly proper to make them explicit—because that would imply that they were propositions amenable to debate and argumentation, rather than simple verities to be accepted. The beliefs "slip from the conscious mind down deep into muscles and glands and become difficult to tear out."[4]

This process of socialization is indispensable for any political society. A society cannot survive or prosper without communicating to its members an understanding of its basic purposes and meaning. If it is unable to do this it will suffer a loss of "legitimacy"; that is to say, if a society cannot convince its members that it is a worthwhile undertaking, it will lose its ability to draw upon their energies and loyalties. When this happens, the society is in trouble. It cannot respond decisively to external threats, and its domestic social order may begin to unravel as well.

This is why political theory, and political theorists, may often seem to be "subversive." Political theory seeks to bring to light the fundamental principles behind political order and to subject them to critical scrutiny. And the critical scrutiny of the operative ideals of a political system may, with good reason, be regarded as unwelcome and potentially dangerous by the powers-that-be. Political theory may challenge the consensus of a society or threaten the legitimacy of an established regime. Far better, from the point of view of established authority, that a society's basic organizing beliefs be accepted as given rather than subjected to serious examination.

Athens put Socrates to death, after all, because he was seen as subversive. His habit of challenging what others took for granted led to his trial and execution. He was charged with "impiety" and "corrupting the young" because he was, in his words, an intellectual "gadfly." The young men who sought him out as a teacher found his questioning of established beliefs provocative and intriguing. But the leadership of the Athenian *polis*, which was in a rather precarious condition, found such questioning offensive and dangerous. They therefore arrested him, hoping to silence him or to make him recant. When they could not succeed in doing so, and he would not consent to be banished, they had him put to death.

So political theory can be a hazardous calling. The questions it raises are not always welcome ones. Totalitarian societies, in fact, undertake strenuous measures to prevent the critical spirit of political theory from ever taking root. They are like secular theocracies, where only "orthodox" ideas are permitted. When it comes to political doctrine, only the official ideology may be promulgated. Questioning the established political dogma is tantamount to heresy.

Liberal societies, such as our own, are more open. They are committed to the principle of free speech, and with this guarantee the serious pursuit of political theory is a possibility. Even here, however, what is welcome in principle may be repugnant in practice. As political science research shows, and as our political history clearly indicates, a people that professes its dedication to "free speech" in the abstract may not be willing to allow "un-American" types to talk in a public forum. Socrates would probably not be too welcome here, either; for like most societies we would rather hear our political system celebrated than hear it questioned.

Because the questions political theory raises can be seen as subversive, and because political theorizing can therefore be dangerous, Leo Strauss has argued that some political theories may need to be read with these facts in mind. A political theorist may have to be very careful about what he says, if he values his health. So you sometimes need to read between the lines to find out his real feelings on the matter.[5]

The resistance of these social and internal "defenses" against political theory tends to weaken significantly in times of crisis. People are much more inclined to question ideas they earlier were content to take for granted when things seem to be falling apart in ways that don't make sense. The powers-that-be may still be inclined to prohibit some kinds of questions as subversive, but more and more people will begin to appreciate the need for some profound attention to the basic rules of the game. The beliefs we have internalized may still be very hard to bring to the light of conscious attention, but it is much more likely that we will begin to recognize them as questionable assumptions when they are causing us distress.

In this country, for example, during the politically calm and quiescent fifties, students of American politics speculated that we might be seeing the "end of ideology." But the stress and turmoil of the late sixties made this speculation unpersuasive—at least for the time being. Disturbed and distressed by Vietnam, by political injustices, or be a decline in the stability, civility, and order of our society, many Americans took a new or renewed interest in political theory. New versions of radical, socialist, and anarchist theories of politics were developed by the "New Left"; liberals were driven to reexamine, to articulate, and to defend their own political philosophy; and conservative political thinkers sought to demonstrate the applicability of their political principles to current problems as well. When the political pot began to boil, the "relevance" of fundamental political beliefs became evident.

The Perception of Disorder

The crises that precipitate political theorizing come in a variety of forms. The crisis may be one that is evident to everyone—at least on the symptomatic level—encompassing the entire society and affecting the lives of all its members. The massive disruptions and calamities that sometimes afflict human society, such as civil war or economic collapse, are the usual examples here. If everyone is at the throat of his neighbor, if all public order and personal safety disappear, if vast numbers are destitute, few people are likely to deny that an urgent problem needs attention.

Even in drastic circumstances like these, however, identifying and understanding the nature of the problem may not be as simple as it seems. Almost everyone may agree *that* something is wrong without agreeing on *what* the problem really is. Widespread civil strife and bloodshed may clearly indicate that a problem exists, for example—but it may be arguable whether the underlying problem is government oppression or government weakness. Take the example of turmoil and confrontation in the sixties referred to above. Almost everyone agreed that these events constituted problems that needed attention. But some saw the problem as "permissiveness" and others saw it as "repression." Complex perceptual judgments come into play very early, even in defining the problem.

Other crises are more limited or subtle, and they may not be so readily apparent to all participants in the political system. Indeed, some may believe that there's really no problem at all, and the theoretical dispute may begin right there. Where Marx saw a problem in the poverty and misery of the British working classes, for example, others saw only the necessary consequences of inevitable laws in an imperfect world. The crisis that generates a political theory, then, may in some cases be more localized and personal than universal. The theorist may become disenchanted or disillusioned with the prevailing ground rules of a political system for reasons which are not clearly visible to all sections of society. He may belong to a group peculiarly disadvantaged by the established assumptions of the society.

Or he may even be a "voice crying in the wilderness" about social injustices or spiritual disintegration which other men cannot or will not see.

Political theory aims, ultimately, at understanding and explaining the *right* order of society. But it originates in a perception that something has gone *wrong*.

Actually, this pattern of discovery, moving from wrong to right, is not unique to political theory. Plenty of examples from everyday experience and from other fields of inquiry suggest that this is a fairly normal way to proceed.

The little bit that I know, for example, about the proper functioning of an automobile engine is largely derived from my encounters with the failures and deficiencies in my own cars. When my engine rapidly and dramatically overheated one day, I learned what a water pump is and what it does. When my car died completely one night for want of any electrical power, I learned what an alternator is and what it does. And from other minor catastrophes more numerous than I care to recall, I have pieced together an understanding of some of the features of a properly functioning automobile. My education through painful experience has been shared, I am sure, by many others.

An eminent student of jurisprudence, Edmond Cahn, has suggested that the same pattern can be found in the area of law. Our conception of justice, he observes, is not something that we arrive at by abstract speculation or by direct thought. We don't sit down and ask, in the abstract, "What is justice?" That problem becomes meaningful to us only through our spontaneous attempts to deal with cases where something strikes us as manifestly *unjust*. We don't deduce norms of just behavior and just law from a priori philosophical principles. We develop them in our attempts to rectify concrete wrongs and to prevent their recurrence.

"Where justice is thought of in the customary manner as an ideal mode or condition, the human response will be merely contemplative," Cahn writes. "But the response to a real or imagined instance of injustice is something quite different; it is alive with movement and warmth in the human organism. ... 'Justice,' as we shall use the term, means the *active process* of remedying or preventing what would arouse the sense of injustice."[6] When men are treated in a way that dramatically violates human dignity, or in a way that is capriciously inequitable, or in a way unrelated to their deserts, the "sense of injustice" is aroused. We react in spontaneous revulsion against such injustices, practically to remedy them and intellectually to set standards of just dealing that will bar their recurrence in the future.

The first question to ask in understanding a political theorist, then, is: "What's his problem?" What does he see that seems wrong or dangerous or corrupt? Why has he been motivated to begin the arduous form of intellectual exploration embodied in writing a profound and coherent political theory? What does he hope to accomplish? What specific failure or disorder does he seek to remedy?

For he almost surely writes in response to a fairly specific and pressing problem of his own society. The account which Walter Lippmann provided of his reason for writing *The Public Philosophy*, in the very first lines of that book, could apply (apart from the geographic specifics) to almost any political theorist. "During the fateful summer of 1938," he wrote, "I began writing a book in an effort *to come to terms in my own mind and heart with the mounting disorder in our Western society*"[7] (italics mine).

This attempt to "come to terms with the mounting disorder in society," as Lippmann put it, usually has an acutely existential side to it. The theorist *experiences* the disorder in his own life, in his own psyche. The problem is "out there" in the society, but it is also "inside" his own person. Social crises disrupt the internal balance of the individuals who are caught up in them. For, as Susanne Langer has said, when "the field of our unconscious symbolic orientation is suddenly plowed up by tremendous changes in the external world and in the social order, we lose our hold, our convictions, and therewith our effectual purposes."[8]

Because the individual psyche is so intimately bound up in social roles, mores, and behavior patterns, derangements in the social order may be experienced in the form of intense emotional confusion and distress. The political theorist may be driven to his reflections on the problems of the body politic in an attempt to locate and dispel the sources of his own psychic suffering. Rousseau, for example, tells us in his *Confessions* about the crucial role his personal anguish played in his political ideas. John Stuart Mill experienced an almost complete emotional collapse which, he relates in his autobiography, led him to see previously unsuspected weaknesses in the rationalistic social ideals he had inherited from his father. And Hegel's personal "identity crisis" seems to have played an important role as a stimulus to his political theory.

In many respects, in fact, political theory can be characterized as a kind of psychotherapy of the body politic. The analogy is a good one in respect to both the structure and the purpose of the inquiry. Like psychotherapy, political theory begins as an attempt to uncover the nature and sources of profound functional disorders. Like psychotherapy, political theory necessitates a deep exploration of the roots of human behavior—areas which have for so long been tacit and taken for granted that they lie beneath the usual range of consciousness. And, like psychotherapy, the ultimate goal of political theory is the restoration of health through confrontation with and triumph over the sources of distress.

Because the political theorist is responding to a specific problem of his own experience does not mean his problem is of purely personal or merely local significance. The value or the relevance of his inquiry derives from his penetration to underlying issues which are *always* present in politics. In examining the problem of civil disruption in seventeenth-century England, for example, Hobbes penetrates to the fundamental and perennial problem of reconciling divergent human desires into a stable society. In examining the corruption of his own eighteenth-century France, Rousseau examines the moral requisites of all human society. In probing the disorders of Renaissance Italy, Machiavelli raises universal questions about the nature and extent of political authority.

A great political theorist, in other words, *transcends* the limitations of his immediate surroundings. His own personal political circumstances raise and define the issues he confronts, but they embody and reflect problems of human order relevant to almost all times and places. Beginning with specific *historical* dilemmas, the theorist worth reading winds up confronting *perennial* questions.

Some of the greatest political theories were written in response to the breakdown, or threatened breakdown, of civil order. They were written at times and places when politics was degenerating into warfare. This immediate and pressing danger forced men like Machiavelli, Hobbes, Burke, and Locke to examine what it is that holds societies together. How and why can men keep their political conflicts and disagreements from tearing apart their societies? No political problem is more fundamental in its practical significance. And no political problem raises more fundamental issues about human nature and the status of society.

A look at some of the concrete circumstances of these epic theorists should clarify and illustrate this recurrent pattern.

Niccolò Machiavelli and a Crisis of Stability

The political circumstances in which Machiavelli wrote, for example, were terribly disordered. For one thing, he was out of a job—a situation which can make anyone aware of the political problems around him. But that was pretty minor. The basic problem was that the city-states of northern Italy around 1500 were in a very bad way. Internally, most of the city-states were very unstable. They seethed with class and factional conflict. Different regimes came and went with great rapidity. Certainly this was the case in Machiavelli's native Florence, which was beset with chronic conflict between the rich and the poor, and between different segments of the aristocracy. Moreover, this internal strife made the city-states very vulnerable to aggression from the outside. Contending armies of the different cities, bands of hired mercenaries, and sometimes the troops of foreign powers such as France crisscrossed the Italian terrain almost continuously.

All in all, it was not a very happy set of political circumstances. In the words of Professor George Sabine, "Italian society and politics [of Machiavelli's day] were peculiarly illustrative of a state of institutional decay. It was a society intellectually brilliant and artistically creative . . . yet it was a prey to the worst political corruption and moral degradation. The older civic institutions were dead. . . . Cruelty and murder had become normal agencies of government; good faith and truthfulness had become childish scruples to which an enlightened man would hardly give lip service; force and craft had become the keys to success; profligacy and debauchery had become too frequent to need comment. . . . It was a period truly called the age of 'bastards and adventurers,' a society created as if to illustrate Aristotle's saying that 'man, when separated from justice, is the worst of all animals.'"[9]

When the Medici family returned to power in Florence in 1512, Machiavelli found himself unemployed, and therefore had time to contemplate the political situation. Machiavelli had, moreover, a good deal of inside knowledge about the ins and outs of Italian politics. As a civil servant of the Florentine government for more than a decade, he had been in a position to see firsthand what went on. He had served on numerous diplomatic missions, for example, where he had the opportunity to watch and analyze the dynamics of dealings among contending political powers.

On the basis of this experience, Machiavelli felt that he had a lot to say about the problems of creating and maintaining viable political regimes. Moreover, he was an avid student of history, so he had thereby added vicarious experience of the politics of other times and places to his own firsthand experience. This knowledge, he thought, had given him the means of understanding the nature and sources of political instability and the means of improving on the situation. He put pen to paper, then, to share these insights with others—to enable them to draw some lessons of their own from the experience of history.

Thomas Hobbes and a Crisis of Authority

A century or so later, England similarly found itself a nation beset by deep political divisions and civil strife. In the first place, English society was torn by bitter religious cleavages. Different political sects, spawned by the Reformation, were locked in battle over issues which spilled over into the political world. A rising commercial middle class was challenging the established privileges of the landed aristocracy. And underlying all of the class, factional, and religious divisions was deep disagreement over the proper constitutional order of the society.

These deep divisions in English society produced a very turbulent political period. The seventeenth century saw one king beheaded, another king restored to the throne after Cromwell's demise, and still another king sent packing by the Parliament and people. The Glorious Revolution, with the Bill of Rights and the Act of Toleration, finally provided a settlement which has proved to be a relatively durable basis for the British political system. But during the course of this very volatile century there were many who wondered whether the English polity might not fall apart altogether.

This crisis of the English political system prompted many thoughtful people in that country to reflect upon the problems that threatened them. They were driven to examine the grounds of political order because the specific political order they inhabited seemed clearly to be very shaky indeed. The noted Anglican thinker Richard Hooker (often cited approvingly as "the judicious Hooker" by Locke) wrote his multivolume *Laws of Ecclesiastical Polity* with the express hope that "posterity may not say that we let it all pass away silently, as if in a dream."

Several of these thinkers succeeded in transcending their immediate circumstances to reach some of the most fundamental problems and principles of all human politics. They were able to see the particular concrete problems which they confronted as manifestations of universal and perennial problems always faced by men engaged in the task of creating a stable and just society. These works, because of their depth, have become classics—contributions to the enduring dialogue of political theory. Despite their immediate concern with the social and constitutional crises faced by post-Reformation England, we can still find them illuminating. Hooker himself, who wrote in the late sixteenth century, is one of these thinkers.

Locke and Thomas Hobbes are even more well known and relevant, because their theories are even less bound up in the particular conventions of their own time and place.

Hobbes expressed his perception of the profound disorder in his society at the outset of his study of the causes of the English civil wars, entitled *Behemoth*. In the period between 1640 and 1660, he wrote, anyone who "should have looked upon the world and observed the actions of men, especially in England, might have had a prospect of all kinds of injustice, and of all kinds of folly, that the world could afford, and how they were produced by their hypocrisy and self-conceit, whereof the one is double iniquity, and the other double folly."[10]

In Hobbes's view, the basic affliction of the English polity was a crisis of *authority*. The people, he wrote, "were corrupted generally." They were "so ignorant of their duty, as that not one perhaps of ten thousand knew what right any man had to command him, or what necessity there was of King or Commonwealth."[11] They had been seduced into this ungovernable condition by ministers, both Catholic and sectarian, who preached the subservience of the temporal power to spiritual authorities, by philosophers who identified monarchy with tyranny, and by other assorted troublemakers.

The result had been the dissolution of the king's sovereign power. And because this cohesive center of authority had been undermined, the British political system teetered on the verge of disintegration. The turmoil and civil warfare of his day, Hobbes believed, was but the foreseeable consequence of this underlying failure of authority. It represented a retrogression into the natural condition of man outside the bonds of civil society, which was a "war of all against all."

John Locke and a Crisis of Legitimacy

Locke saw England's political disorder rather differently. The British monarchy had indeed lost much of its authority, he agreed. But this loss of authority had come about, in his view, because the monarchy had tried to exceed the scope of its authority. The real crisis, then, was a crisis of *legitimacy*. It was not that the people had been corrupted or disobedient because of their natural perversity, or because they had been seduced by false prophets. It was that the rulers of the society had tried to seize and exercise powers not properly theirs. The people, in short, had good reason for their behavior. They were resisting political usurpation.

Locke elaborated this perception of the crisis of British politics by discussing the relationship of rulers and ruled in terms of a contract. Since men are free, equal, and rational by nature, Locke argued, they could not be supposed to have submitted themselves to any arbitrary and absolute power. Instead, government is by its very nature a fiduciary trust, dependent upon the authorization and consent of the governed, and circumscribed by clear limitations. Whenever the rulers of a given society try to take powers which have not been granted to them, they dissolve the contract between themselves and the people; and the people are thereby released from their obligations to obey.

The crisis of his own society, Locke believed, was of precisely this kind. The rulers of England had ruptured the contractual relationship with their subjects by reaching for powers not rightly theirs—by taxing without consent, by creating armies without authorization, and by conniving against the religious liberties of the people.

Clearly, underlying these conflicting perceptions by Hobbes and Locke of the constitutional breakdown in England were some deeper differences. Most immediately, the one's perception of an authority crisis and the other's depiction of a crisis of legitimacy rested upon opposing views as to the "true origin, extent and end of civil government"—the subtitle of Locke's justly famous and influential *Second Treatise of Civil Government.* And this dispute, in turn, rested upon their profoundly different assessments of human nature and of the necessities of politics. As they were forced to explain and to justify their contrasting perceptions of the crisis of English society, therefore, Locke and Hobbes were pushed into developing their very penetrating and influential theoretical visions of politics.

The Philosophes and the Crisis of the Ancien Régime

The turbulent political decades surrounding the French Revolution, just like the revolutionary period in England, generated some important political theorizing. The crisis of French society, which sent tremors throughout Europe, forced both advocates and opponents of the revolution to reflect deeply about the necessities and possibilities of politics.

The condition of the *ancien régime* in France clearly grew increasingly critical as the eighteenth century wore on. The monarchy, tied to an anachronistic feudal aristocracy, grew ever more ineffective in its policies and ever more out of touch with the people. This crisis of effectiveness and legitimacy demanded explanation. The misery and alienation that it caused, especially among the lower ranks of the society, seemed evident. But what was the underlying nature of the problem?

In the eyes of the liberal *philosophes* the political difficulties in France were symptomatic of a deeper social and intellectual crisis in Western civilization. They saw history as an epic saga of reason, the story, as Condorcet put it, of the progress of the human mind. And the advance of reason brought with it the enlargement of human freedom. Truth and liberty developed hand in hand. Yet each advance in reason was opposed by those who had a vested interest in maintaining established systems of privilege. Truth and liberty were always opposed by entrenched forces of tyranny and superstition.

For the *philosophes*, then, the crisis of the *ancien régime* was but the latest and penultimate episode in this perennial confrontation. The religious authorities, who were interested in retaining their power over people's minds, and the political authorities, who wished to maintain control over people's bodies, had coalesced to fight the tide of liberty and rationality. Humanity would become free, as one *philosophe* wrote mordantly, only when the last king was hanged by the entrails of the last priest.

When the French Revolution swept aside the debris of the *ancien régime* and established a new social order, then, many people enthusiastically foresaw the advent of a bright new political age. Across the Channel, in England, for example, some prominent religious leaders and intellectuals began to argue and organize in behalf of the principles of the revolution. They hoped to transplant these principles onto English soil and to duplicate the achievements of the French revolutionaries in their own country.

Edmund Burke and a Crisis of Civility

This scenario may have appealed to some, but the prominent English statesman Edmund Burke found it a terrifying prospect. The "solution" to the human political predicament allegedly afforded by the revolutionary new order he saw as the beginning of yet another crisis. He was moved, therefore, to write his own major work of political theory, his *Reflections on the Revolution in France*. He hoped in that work to alert his countrymen to the dangers and follies he saw in the new regime in France, and thereby to save them from falling into the same plight. "It appears to me," he wrote, "as if I were in a great crisis, not of the affairs of France alone, but of all of Europe, perhaps of more than Europe.... The beginnings of confusion with us in England are at present feeble enough, but ... we have seen an infancy still more feeble growing by moments into a strength to heap mountains upon mountains and to wage war with heaven itself. Whenever our neighbor's house is on fire, it cannot be amiss for the engines to play a little on our own."[12]

The French, Burke contended, thought they had laid the foundations of a truly free society. But this belief was a delusion. Instead, by destroying all the social bases of ordered liberty, such as religion, chivalric manners, and social hierarchy, France had thrown overboard essential restraints on licentious passions. Corruption, mediocrity, and, in the longer run, an oscillation between tyranny and anarchy would be the result, he predicted. In his highly rhetorical style, Burke sketched the outlines of this crisis: "France has bought undisguised calamities at a higher price than any nation has purchased the most unequivocal blessings! France has bought poverty by crime! France has not sacrificed her virtue to her interest, but she has abandoned her interest, that she might prostitute her virtue. . . . France, when she let loose the reins of regal authority, doubled the license of a ferocious dissoluteness in manners and of an insolent irreligion in opinions and practice, and has extended through all ranks of life, as if she were communicating some privilege or laying open some secluded benefit, all the unhappy corruptions that usually were the disease of wealth and power."[13]

Karl Marx and the Crisis of Capitalism

Writing during another turbulent period, around the revolutions of 1848, and looking from another end of the political spectrum, Karl Marx saw a different kind of disorder threatening European society. The economic engine of capitalist society was very powerful, he perceived. It was successful in creating goods more proficiently than any previous system. In doing so, however, it created a new and ominous derangement in the social life of the men who worked within it. Some of the more obvious evidence of this derangement, Marx felt, was readily apparent—in the poverty and misery of the working class. But for various reasons men had not appreciated or understood the *significance* of these problems; and they seemed unaware, in Marx's view, of some of the deeper dimensions of the difficulty.

This failure of perception, this lack of consciousness or awareness of the situation, Marx hoped to remedy. The goal of his political theory was to help men understand their predicament. His task consisted "in enabling the world to clarify its consciousness, in waking it from its dream about itself, in explaining to it the meaning of its own actions."[14] Men would then be able to cooperate with the historical forces at work to overcome the problem, rather than struggling vainly and self-destructively against these forces. Marx even went so far as to say that "to have its sins forgiven mankind has only to declare them to be what they really are."[15]

These "sins" which Marx perceived and sought to "declare" were the *alienation* of labor and the *contradictions* of bourgeois society.

Bourgeois society, Marx believed, contained many contradictions—internal tensions and inconsistencies. At the most basic level, though, the main contradiction he saw was between the riches that capitalism could produce and the human impoverishment it in fact created. "It is true," he wrote, "that labor produces for the rich wonderful things—but for the worker it produces privation. It produces palaces—but for the worker, hovels. It produces beauty—but for the worker, deformity. It replaces labor by machines—but some of the workers it throws back to a barbarous type of labor, and the other workers it turns into machines. It produces intelligence—but for the worker idiocy, cretinism." [16]

The system of production and distribution embodied by a capitalist society, Marx argued, alienated and estranged man. It alienated him, first of all, from the products he created. The work of his own hands and spirit was taken from him and confronted him as "an alien object exercising power over him." The objects or goods which he created did not belong to him. They became instead "an alien world antagonistically opposed to him." [17] Man was therefore alienated from "nature"—that is, the objects in the world—by the capitalist mode of production.

Moreover, Marx continued, man was also estranged from himself in the same process. Not only the *products* of his labor, but also that *activity* of labor as well, fell under the control of external forces. The worker found "his own activity as an alien activity not belonging to him; it is activity as suffering, strength as weakness, begetting as emasculating, the worker's *own* physical and mental energy, his personal life or that is life other than activity—as an activity which is turned against him, neither depends on nor belongs to him. Here we have *self-estrangement*, as we had previously the estrangement of the thing." [18]

And finally, Marx continued, the capitalist system estranges man from his fellows. Man is essentially a "species-being," Marx wrote—a rather abstract way of saying that man is a communal as well as an individual being. Man exists as a part of a group, in relationship and interaction with other men, and not merely as a single, isolable individual. And this aspect of man's being—his relationship to the life of his species—was also disrupted and distorted by bourgeois society. Man was alienated not only from nature and from himself, but from other men as well.

Jean-Jacques Rousseau and a Crisis of Moral Equality

Rousseau's quest for the good society also began with his perception of human alienation and underlying contradictions in his society, although he did not use that language exactly, and he didn't see things in quite the same way as Marx.

The "alienation" which he saw afflicting his fellow man— and himself!—referred principally to the last two of Marx's three types of alienation: estrangement from one's true self and from one's fellow man. Man's self-estrangement, as Rousseau saw it, was a kind of socially induced phoniness. The manners and mores of the day led men to repress their natural sentiments—to bury them beneath artificial forms and conventions that were constraining and crippling. "There prevails in modern manners," he wrote, "a servile and deceptive conformity; so that one would think every mind had been cast in the same mold. Politeness requires this thing; decorum that; ceremony has its forms, and fashion its laws, and these we must always follow, never the promptings of our own nature. We no longer dare seem what we really are, but lie under a perpetual restraint." [19]

This repression at the individual level, this estrangement of man from himself, in turn brought about a dislocation of man's social relations, Rousseau averred. "What a train of vices must attend this uncertainty! Sincere friendship, real esteem, and perfect confidence are banished from among men. Jealousy, suspicion, fear, coldness, reserve, hate and fraud lie constantly concealed under that uniform and deceitful veil of politeness; that boasted candor and urbanity, for which we are indebted," said Rousseau ironically, "to the light and leading of this age. We shall no longer take in vain by our oaths the name of our Creator; but we shall insult Him with our blasphemies, and our scrupulous ears will take no offence. We have grown too modest to brag of our own deserts; but we do not scruple to decry those of others."[20] And so on.

The moral disorder which Rousseau perceived in his society had its expressly political, governmental dimension as well. Moral derangement and political corruption went together. Rousseau expressed his perception of the latter in one of his most famous passages. In his "Discourse on the Origin of Inequality" he wrote: "Moral inequality, authorized by positive right alone, clashes with natural right, whenever it is not proportionate to physical inequality—a distinction which sufficiently determines what we ought to think of that species of inequality which prevails in all civilized countries; since it is plainly contrary to the law of nature, however defined, that children should command old men, fools wise men, and that the privileged few should gorge themselves with superfluities, while the starving multitude are in want of the bare necessities of life."[21]

As the examples of Burke, Marx, and Rousseau suggest, the political disorders which the theorist sees may go beyond the outright collapse of physical security. They may involve the more subtle and complex domain of the society's moral order. A genuinely unjust or repressive political regime is always in some jeopardy because it risks the erosion of its claim to legitimacy. But it is certainly possible for a society to maintain law and order successfully while nonetheless perpetuating morally perverse social arrangements that blight and constrict the lives of its citizens.

Plato and the Crisis of Athenian Justice

One of the best examples of a political theorist's attempt to illuminate a disorder of this kind is also one of the earliest. For Plato, who is generally considered to be the founder of the Western tradition of political theory, wrote one of his dialogues specifically to express his sense of the moral perversity of his own society.

The bankruptcy of the Athenian *polis*, Plato believed, was brought into sharp relief by a real-life drama. This was the trial and execution of Socrates, who was for Plato, and for many others, one of the finest and wisest men the world had known. Yet the city of Athens arrested him, put him on trial, and finally condemned him to death.

For Plato, the trial of Socrates was actually a trial of Athenian society. In deciding what it should do about Socrates, Athens was actually deciding, or perhaps revealing, something about its own "soul." It was deciding whether its own political order could be a home for this wise and virtuous citizen or whether Athens was incapable of permitting the kind of life which Socrates embodied. And when the Athenian court (the "jury" was composed of five hundred Athenian citizens) condemned Socrates, they were in reality condemning themselves.

To convey his perception of the disorder of Athenian society, therefore, Plato simply converted the real-life drama of Socrates' trial into a more stylized literary drama. In the *Apology*, Plato refined and polished the judicial confrontation of Socrates with his accusers into an indictment of Athenian society.

The *Apology* is systematically ironic. Each stage of the trial takes place on two levels. At the superficial level, Athens puts Socrates on trial, convicts him, and sentences him to death. On a deeper level, however, the moral order of the cosmos, embodied in the soul of Socrates, puts Athens on trial and finds it wanting.

In the first part of the dialogue, Athens accuses Socrates of impiety and corrupting the young. In response, Socrates accuses Athens of attacking him because it cannot bear the truth to which his life is devoted. The oracle at Delphi, Socrates relates, once declared him, Socrates, to be the wisest of men. Puzzled by this praise, because he realized how little he knew, Socrates finally understood, he says, that the oracle "only made use of my name, and took me as an example, as though he would say to men, 'He among you is the wisest who, like Socrates, knows that his wisdom is really worth nothing at all.'"[22]

Therefore, Socrates continues, he had gone about Athens "testing and examining every man whom I think wise, whether he be a citizen or a stranger, as the god has commanded me. Whenever I find that he is not wise, I point out to him, in the god's behalf, that he is not wise."[23] In so doing, Socrates contends, he has in fact performed a real service to Athens, as well as to his *daimon*. He has been like a "gadfly" to a sluggish horse that needs to be aroused. But, understandably, his service has not made him popular among those who cannot bear the truth. "For I suppose," says Socrates, "they would not like to confess the truth, which is that they are shown up as ignorant pretenders to knowledge that they do not possess."[24]

Broadening his indictment of the Athenian polis, Socrates says that his devotion to the truth has kept him from participation in politics. Politics, as practiced in Athens, is incompatible with the truth—and, therefore, hostile to it. No genuinely truthful man could survive Athenian politics. "Athenians, it is quite certain that, if I had attempted to take part in politics, I should have perished at once and long ago without doing any good either to you or to myself. And do not be indignant with me for telling the truth. There is no man who will preserve his life for long, either in Athens or elsewhere, if he firmly opposes the multitude, and tries to prevent the commission of much injustice and illegality in the state."[25]

After this very unrepentant defense, Socrates is found guilty. He then, by customary Athenian practice, could propose an alternative punishment to that proposed by the prosecution. And here the ironic contrast of the truth with the corruption of Athens continues. As Socrates observes, if his fate is to be *just* it should be what he *deserves.* And since he has provided a valuable service to the society, his "punishment" should be something good. Faced with the prosecution's request of a death penalty, Socrates proposes that instead he should receive free meals in the civic dining hall—an honor usually bestowed upon local heroes such as victors in the Olympic games. His proposal is a funny one in the context of the *official* meaning of the trial. But in the context of the *real,* deeper meaning of the confrontation, his proposal makes good sense. Indeed, it is a perfectly fitting response. For, as Socrates says, "when I am persuaded that I have never wronged any man, I shall certainly not wrong myself, or admit that I deserve to suffer any evil, or propose any evil for myself as a penalty. Why should I?"[26]

The Athenian jury of five hundred citizens then condemns Socrates to death. Once again, however, Plato makes it clear that the real condemnation runs the other way around. In pronouncing sentence upon Socrates, Athens has in fact confessed its own moral failure. Socrates, in the dialogue, points this out. "But, my friends, I think that it is a much harder thing to escape from wickedness than from death, for wickedness is swifter than death. And now I, who am old and slow, have been overtaken by the slower pursuer: and my accusers, who are clever and swift, have been overtaken by the swifter pursuer—wickedness. And now I shall go away, sentenced by you to death; they will go away, sentenced by truth to wickedness and injustice. And I abide by this award as well as they. Perhaps it was right for these things to be so. I think that they are fairly balanced." [27]

Plato's political theory could be said to "begin"—that is, to have its philosophical foundations—in one of a number of areas. It could be said to have its foundations in his cosmology, or in his epistemology, or in his philosophical anthropology (his view of "human nature"). His basic philosophical premises are interrelated, and they touch all of these areas. The dynamic starting point of his political theory, however—its origin in his logic-in-use—lies right here in the *Apology*. The impetus for his analysis of political order arises from the stark contrast that Plato sees there between the true order, balance, justice, and harmony of the Socratic soul and the official "order" of the Athenian polis. This is the problem that torments him personally and challenges him intellectually. Plato is driven, both "logically" and emotionally, by the perception of political disorder conveyed in the *Apology* to confront the questions of the *Republic*: What is justice? What is the good society? At the minimum, what kind of social order would not cannibalize its best citizens as Athens had done to Socrates? At the maximum, what kind of social order would be truly a home for a good man?

In short, Plato, like most political theorists, begins his inquiry with a "perception of disorder" in the body politic. To see something as "wrong" presents an intellectual problem, discovers an anomaly that needs explanation. At the same time, to see something as wrong provides the existential motivation that impels one to push on toward a solution: it stirs the passions as well as the mind.

Some political theorists are much more explicit about this perception of disorder than others. Plato, for example, is unusually specific about it since he uses it as the basis for a whole dialogue. Other theorists may not provide an account of the original problem that motivated their examination of political order, or they may bury it in an early, less widely read fragment of their work. In the case of Marx, for example, one needs to look at some of his earlier pieces, such as the "Economic and Philosophic Manuscripts of 1844," to get a good idea of what is bothering him—of what he sees as basically wrong in the politics of his time. Or one may simply have to understand and appreciate the concrete situation which provided the context in which the theorist wrote—to appreciate the political chaos of Machiavelli's Italy, for example.

Even if it takes a little digging, then, it is worthwhile making the effort to identify the fundamental perception of disorder that motivates any political theorist. Unless he began with a *problem*, a political theorist probably wouldn't have bothered to write. And unless we can appreciate this problem, we are not likely to understand the answer which the completed theory tries to provide.

NOTES

[1] Quoted by Daniel Boorstin, *The Genius of American Politics* (Chicago: University of Chicago Press, 1953), p. 3.

[2] Louis Hartz, *The Liberal Tradition in America* (New York: Harcourt Brace, 1955), p. 11.

[3] Lillian Smith, *Killers of the Dream* (Garden City, N.Y.: Doubleday, 1963), pp. 17, 19, 75.

[4] Ibid., p. 81.

[5] See, for example, Leo Strauss, *Persecution and the Art of Writing* (New York: The Free Press, 1952).

[6] Edmond Cahn, *The Sense of Injustice* (Bloomington, Indiana: Indiana University Press, 1949), pp. 13-14.

[7] Walter Lippmann, The Public Philosophy (New York: Mentor Books, 1956), p. 11.

[8] Susanne K. Langer, Philosophy in a New Key (New York: Mentor Books, 1951), p. 245.

[9] George Sabine, A History of Political Theory, rev. ed. (New York: Henry Holt, 1950), pp. 337-38.

[10] Thomas Hobbes, Behemoth (New York: Burt Franklin, 1963), p. 3.

[11] Ibid., pp. 4, 6-7.

[12] Edmund Burke, Reflections on the Revolution in France (New York: Liberal Arts Press, 1955), pp. 11 and 10.

[13] Ibid., pp. 42-43.

[14] Karl Marx, "For a Ruthless Criticism to Everything Existing" in Robert C. Tucker, ed., The Marx-Engels Reader (New York: Norton, 1972), p. 10.

[15] Ibid.

[16] Karl Marx, Economic and Philosophic Manuscripts of 1844, in Tucker, ed., The Marx-Engels Reader, p. 59.

[17] Ibid., p. 60.

[18] Ibid., p. 61.

[19] Jean-Jacques Rousseau, "A Discourse on the Arts and Sciences," in Rousseau, The Social Contract and Discourses, translated by G. D. H. Cole (New York: E. P. Dutton, 1950), p. 149.

[20] Ibid.

[21] Rousseau, "A Discourse on the Origin of Inequality," in Social Contract and Discourses, pp. 271-72.

[22] Plato, Apology, translated by F. J. Church and revised by Robert D. Cumming (Indianapolis: Bobbs-Merrill, 1958), p. 28.

[23] Ibid.

[24] Ibid.

[25] Ibid., p. 38.

[26] Ibid., p. 44.

[27] Ibid., p. 46.

THREE

DIAGNOSIS

Only a very strange human mind could rest content with the perception of disorder. Both mind and heart push onward. The natural impetus of the dynamic "logic" of perception and the natural concern of a troubled spirit lead on to further inquiry. The solution to the very first problem—"What is going wrong here?"—creates new puzzlement of its own. The answer given by the perception of disorder is the embryo of more questions.

The passions that prompted the theorist's original investigation are still alive, because no remedy for the perceived disorder has been found at this stage. The basic problem has simply been identified, not solved. The mere perception of what is wrong offers no practical guidance. The existential disquiet which caused the theorist to begin thinking has not been dispelled. He must continue his inquiry in order to find out how to handle his predicament—to know what he must do.

The intellectual impetus of the inquiry is also still very much present. When the theorist perceives something as *dis*-ordered, the logic of perception demands that the context of this perception be filled in. Two questions in particular immediately arise. First, if the situation is disordered, *why* is it in such a state? And second, if this political situation is disordered, what would a *well-ordered* system look like? If this be "wrong," then what is "right"?

The second of these questions will be confronted in the next chapter. In this chapter, we shall look at the problems and processes which confront the political theorist when he asks the former question—when he wants to discover *why* the unsatisfactory state of affairs he sees has come about.

Causes and Cures

The intellectual problems here are essentially those found in the study of any form of pathology. The political theorist who has identified a malfunction in the body politic is in pretty much the same position as the doctor who has identified the symptoms of a disease. Neither can stop at that point. Locating the symptom is not enough; the ailment must be traced back to its *source.* The causes of the problem must be found if the trouble is to be understood, theoretically. And the same thing must happen if the trouble is to be treated, practically. In short, the political theorist, like the physician, is faced with the task of *diagnosis.*

At this stage of his inquiry, the political theorist must become a causal analyst. He is inescapably faced with the very tricky task of trying to sort out cause-and-effect relationships in a very complex world. For unless he can identify the causes of the problem he has perceived, he really doesn't understand it. And unless he knows the causes, he cannot make any well-founded suggestions for curing, or alleviating, the problem.

The very first question which the theorist confronts when he begins his diagnosis is one of the most crucial issues in all of political theory. It is a very difficult question to answer. It is a question which divides important schools of political thinking. And it is a question whose answer profoundly shapes the prescriptive conclusions of any political theorist.

This crucial initial question can be stated rather simply— but it requires some careful elaboration and explanation. The question is: Does the political problem at issue have a political source? Is the cause as well as the symptom genuinely political?

This crucial question breaks down into two others. For a "political" cause is one that is *general* rather than *individual;* and it is one that is *artificial* rather than *natural.* Therefore, the theorist must discover whether the source of his problem is one that arises at the level of society—and is thus a general one—or whether it is merely an affliction of his own personality. And then, if he decides that it is a general social problem, he must decide whether it is the product of humanly changeable arrangements—a problem of convention—or whether it is a "given" of nature.

We shall soon see why this diagnostic issue is a very difficult one that marks a watershed between different schools of political theorists. But the importance of this question for the final prescriptive suggestions of the theorist should already be apparent. For if the cause of a problem is not political in nature—if the cause is not general and conventional—then the appropriate remedy for that problem is not likely to be political either. If the cause is not political, then political responses may still be necessary, but responses at that level could not reasonably be expected to eliminate the problem.

General vs. Individual Problems

Consider the first question that arises in deciding whether the source of a problem is "political": Is the problem a general, social problem or is it merely a personal, idiosyncratic problem? Is it a problem with the system, or is it an individual hang-up? Does the source of the trouble lie in the political arrangements of the society or does it grow out of a personal neurosis? Clearly, the answer makes a big difference. For if the problem is with the system, then political action is probably the appropriate response. But if it's merely an individual psychic disorder, then it's the theorist's personal problem and not really a political issue. He should climb down off his soapbox and go to see a psychiatrist or a minister. He should put down his placard and examine the state of his psyche or soul.

This question is not an easy one to adjudicate. It is by no means a simple matter to decide whether a problem in human life is a problem of the self or of society. For self and society are alter egos. Society is a system of relationships among selves; and individual selves grow out of social interaction. It's not easy to know where one begins and the other ends—or to know whether a breakdown originates with the self or with the society.

What shows up as a personal, psychic disruption may in fact be the result of distorted and dehumanizing social patterns.

As human beings, we attain our identity in large part through the internalization of social roles. We learn who we are by looking in the mirror of society. And if the role assigned us is charged with negative overtones, then we are likely to develop a bad self-image. Recalling his youth, for example, the black writer James Baldwin once remembered that he "was always being mercilessly scrubbed and polished, as in the hope that a stain could thus be washed away. I hazard," he continued, "that the Negro children, of my generation anyway, had an earlier and more painful acquaintance with soap than any other children, anywhere." Such a child learned quickly that his skin color was considered a personal stigma. If he accepted this stigma, he could be psychically damaged by a loss of necessary self-esteem. And if he rejected the stigma he was forced to be more aggressive than he would normally have been—to suffer from "black rage." In either case, his "inner" psychological difficulties could rather clearly be seen as caused by a political derangement.

Or, to take another example, consider the psychological makeup of the modern man who has internalized what Erich Fromm calls the "marketing orientation" of some modern societies. Fromm argues, in an analysis similar to Marx's analysis of alienation, that such a man suffers from coming to see himself as a "commodity": "Human qualities like friendliness, courtesy, kindness, are transformed into commodities, into assets of the 'personality package,' conducive to a higher price on the personality market. If the individual fails in a profitable investment of himself, he feels that *he* is a failure; if he succeeds, *he* is a success. Clearly, his sense of his own value always depends on factors extraneous to himself, on the fickle judgment of the market, which decides about his value as it decides about the value of commodities. . . . The alienated personality who is for sale must lose a good deal of the sense of dignity which is so characteristic of man even in most primitive cultures."[1]

On the other hand, problems that seem rather clearly to stem from the psychological makeup of an individual, or a group of individuals, may be blamed inaccurately upon society. This is the phenomenon that psychologists call "projection." Those who always see conspirators lurking around every corner, for example, may be trying to find objective justification for their irrational anxieties and insecurity. They feel threatened, so they see a political threat—whether it be in an "international Jewish conspiracy" or in a fascist conspiracy of the Rockefellers. Paranoia seeks a political outlet and a political warrant.

Similarly, psychological problems may intrude into politics via the mechanisms of "transference" and "displacement." Transference occurs when a person perceives, and responds to, another individual he really doesn't know as if that person were someone else he does know. Usually this happens when a person transfers the perceptions and responses he has had in regard to a parent to some third party—as for example when he sees his psychiatrist (or a teacher or a minister) as a "father figure." Someone in authority is perceived as though he were the original authority figure, the parent, in a person's life. This often seems to happen in the case of political authorities, for understandable reasons. The excessive veneration and the equally excessive hostility shown toward almost all prominent political authority figures—in our own country the president is the leading case in point—undoubtedly stem in part from this psychological mechanism. A political assassin may even be motivated in part by a repressed desire to destroy his own father. Demons spawned in the individual psyche or in the individual family may thus be loosed on the political stage.

In displacement, the individual similarly shifts some of his feelings and actions around in ways that can have political consequences. Angered by a nagging wife or a carping boss, or frustrated by failures in any of life's endeavors, an individual often finds an outlet for his pent-up hostilities in aggressive behavior toward others—even though these others were not at all responsible for his problems. This psychological mechanism helps the individual blow off steam. But it can become a political problem when specific groups in society, or other nations perhaps, become targeted as acceptable targets for this kind of resentment. In that case, once again, the political turmoil of wars or race riots may be spawned, or at least worsened, by forces which arise from within the psyche.

We can see, then, that self and society are intimately intertwined in multiple and complex ways. Social disorders can cause psychological derangements and vice versa. Causation here may be very difficult to determine. However difficult it may be, though, a political theorist must make some judgments on these very thorny issues of cause and effect in the course of his diagnosis. And the answers he comes up with at this stage of his inquiry are likely to be crucial for his whole theory.

The first task of the theorist is to be sure that the sources of the problem he perceives are political and not merely personal. He must be sure that his perception of political disorder is not simply a product of his own projection or transference or displacement. Crucial disagreements among contending political analyses often develop right at this point.

Take, for example, the notion of "alienation" so important to Hegelian and Marxian social theory. For Hegel, alienation— or estrangement from self—was a cosmic phenomenon. Politics was for him, in fact, the story of God's overcoming his estrangement from himself in history. Alienation was a very real thing, "out there" in the "objective" world. Some of Hegel's critics have countered, on the other hand, by accusing him of psychological projection. The picture he elaborated of an alienated deity struggling to become infinite, to become wholly free and omniscient, was in fact a projection of Hegel's own neurotic self, they maintain. What Hegel diagnosed as a universal political tension, these critics argue, was in fact a fundamental tension in his own Faustian psyche.[2]

One of these critics, Professor Robert Tucker, goes on to argue that two of Hegel's most famous and important followers—Feuerbach and Marx—also provided faulty diagnoses of alienation. Feuerbach saw alienation as a product of religion: man projects his ideal self onto a being he calls God, and thereby becomes alienated from himself. Marx saw alienation as a consequence of capitalism: man becomes alienated from himself and from other men through the money worship and division of labor which capitalism brings about. Both diagnoses, in Tucker's view, are wrong:

> They were both mistaken. Not only did they respectively misread Christianity and capitalism; they failed to grasp the essence of self-alienation. In its intrinsic nature, this is neither a fact of religion nor a fact of political economy. It may find expression in

the economic life or in religion, just as it may also find expression in politics, war and every other human pursuit. Thus, a given alienated individual may develop a compulsive urge towards absolute enrichment, and for him the economic life will indeed be a practical religion of money-worship and a sphere of "alienated labor." But his alienation only becomes in a derivative way an economic fact. Inherently or in itself it is a fact of the life of the self, i.e. a spiritual or, as we say today, psychological fact. It is a *sickness of the self* growing out of and reflecting a man's confusion of humanity in his own person with deity, his quest to actualize himself as a super-human absolute being. Alienation is the counterpart of egoism in this sense. It is not, therefore, a general condition of humanity. Man is not born alienated, although he is born with a potentiality of becoming an alienated individual. No matter how many individual men may belong to this category, *it is always an individual matter.*[3] (Italics mine.)

Marx, Feuerbach, and Tucker, then, all perceive the existence of alienation in human life. But they diagnose the sources of the ailment very differently. The contrasting analyses of Marx and Tucker, especially, illuminate the point at issue here. For Marx sees alienation as a political and economic problem, a product of the social system. Tucker, on the other hand, sees alienation as a psychological or spiritual problem, a product of the inordinate aspirations of the human ego.

The programmatic implications of these different diagnoses clearly diverge. If alienation is a problem caused by the social structure, then the obvious answer is to change that social structure. As Marx said, the point is not simply to understand the world but to *change* it. Only by altering the system, only by concrete political action, can the problem be successfully confronted. But if Tucker's diagnosis of the problem is correct, Marx's political program is quite beside the point. Trying to solve alienation by changing the social order is, if alienation is an attribute of the individual psyche, rather like trying to heal a heart condition with a splint. The proper prescription from Tucker's point of view is not to change the world, but rather to heed the Socratic admonition: Know thyself! The first diagnosis of the situation points toward revolution; the other, toward a kind of repentance.

The same diagnostic disagreement—that is, as to whether a social disorder was a systemic political problem or an individual psychological problem—surfaced in disputation surrounding student radicalism in the sixties. In his indictment of "the system," a prominent student radical charged that "we [the students] have you [the establishment] to blame for our hangups." The "inner" conflicts and psychic pain of young people today, he alleged, are caused by the attempt to adjust to a system which is repressive and dehumanizing. To which Anna Freud, among others, responded by saying: "Baloney!" Don't blame your growing pains, which are a normal and necessary part of psychological maturation, on us! the young radicals were told. As one critic put it, they were "turning adolescence into an ideology," trying to make a political issue out of a problem of psychological development. Again, the implications of these conflicting accounts obviously diverge. If the first analysis is correct, the solution becomes "Change the system!"; whereas if the second analysis is correct, the solution simply becomes "Grow up!"

"Are you a part of the problem," the popular query goes, "or a part of the solution?" By now it should be clear that that depends on what you see as the problem. And that very tricky judgment is one of the crucial stages of inquiry in political theory.

Natural vs. Artificial Causes

A parallel diagnostic problem (indeed, a partly overlapping problem) is the second question mentioned earlier: Is the source of disorder *natural* or *artificial?* Does the problem grow out of "given" and inescapable features of the world—to which man must simply adjust himself? Or does it grow out of aspects of the world which man has created himself—and hence which he could change or alter if he saw fit to do so? Are the causes of human and social unhappiness rooted in the "nature of things"? Or are they rooted in parts of our environment that we can control?

A prayer attributed to Reinhold Niebuhr is appropriate for the political theorist as he enters this stage of his inquiry: "Oh,

Lord, give me the courage to change those things that I can change, the patience to accept those things that I cannot change, and the wisdom to know the difference."

The last of these virtues is especially necessary for the political theorist. He need not excel in courage: Hobbes, who allegedly was born a bit prematurely when his mother was shocked to hear of the approach of the Spanish Armada, once ascribed his own timidity to his being "twin-born with fear." Nor need he be especially patient: many theorists have been passionately eager for change. But, as one who claims insight into the human political condition, the political theorist clearly must possess the "wisdom to know the difference" between those political problems which are soluble and those which must be endured as part of man's fate.

For if he errs at this point of his inquiry, he can compound people's political troubles rather than alleviate them. On the one hand, if his analysis wrongly identifies certain evils as curable when they are not, those who heed his theory are likely to undertake the impossible. His illusions will generate political folly. His followers will be like King Canute, who vainly commanded the tide to stop rising. But while the king merely drenched himself in brine, more violent political follies produced by a similar diagnostic error may drench whole peoples in blood.

On the other hand, an analysis which wrongly identifies genuine evils as incurable has its real costs, as well. The theorist who designates as "natural" and beyond human control problems that social action could in fact alleviate condemns people to suffer unnecessarily. He discourages possible and desirable social reform. If heeded, his faulty diagnosis can exact a heavy price.

Broadly speaking, more "conservative" political theorists tend to see human unhappiness as stemming more from natural causes than from political failures. Or, perhaps the relationship is better expressed the other way around: a theorist who perceives the principal sources of human unhappiness as natural will tend to be more conservative in his ultimate political outlook than the theorist who perceives the principal sources of human unhappiness as social. This relationship is quite logical.

For if people suffer principally from forces beyond human control, then it is hardly rational to expect politics to make them happy. But if people suffer mostly from faulty political arrangements, then political action becomes the appropriate place to look for relief.

The rational conservative, in other words, believes with Peter Berger that "human beings suffer for many reasons and much of this suffering is not amenable to mitigation by political means. One of the severe shortcomings of contemporary 'pan-politicalism' is a failure to understand this—a failure that is finally due to a (probably deliberate) avoidance of the reality of human finitude and mortality."[4] The corresponding "radical" diagnosis points an accusatory finger at "the system." Richard Neuhaus reflects this position when he argues, contra Berger's emphasis, that "all these problems are symptomatic of a more fundamental corruption. . . . The point is that the evil is inherent in, and not accidental to, the American Way. . . . The System itself must be changed."[5]

Similarly, radical diagnosis tends to assign responsibility for "personal problems" to social causes. The radical diagnosis, in fact, tends to minimize the analytical distinction between the self and society. Herbert Marcuse, for example, argues that "the traditional borderlines between psychology on the one hand and political and social philosophy on the other have been made obsolete by the condition of man in the present era."[6] Thus, psychological symptoms may be taken as manifestations of disorder which is fundamentally political: "Psychological problems therefore turn into political problems: private disorder reflects more directly than before the total disorder of the whole, and the cure of personal disorder depends more directly than before on the cure of the general disorder."[7]

And, on this view, if people don't generally perceive that the cause of their problems is basically political, that ignorance represents a failure of consciousness. In fact, it may reflect a form of "brainwashing" by the system. For example, the American socialist Michael Lerner argues that "Americans have been heavily indoctrinated to believe that the problems they feel are not social, but personal, and reflect their own inner difficulties. When they sense something wrong with their lives, they are instructed to look inward, whether through the old forms of religion or psychoanalysis, or the more hip version of encounter groups."[8] Religion is, on this view, an opiate of the people cognitively as well as emotionally. It offers a false and misleading analysis of man's predicament.

In contrast, the more conservative theorist finds the radical diagnosis trivial and misleading. In his view, the attempt to lay the blame for one's personal troubles on the doorstep of society is wrong both intellectually and morally. It is wrong intellectually because such a view provides a faulty and superficial account of the human psyche; and it is wrong morally because it seeks to use "society" as an excuse to abdicate responsibility for one's own weaknesses.

Some of the classic confrontations among political theorists turn around these diagnostic issues.

The Problem of Ignorance: Thomas Paine vs. Edmund Burke

One very famous clash between divergent views of society, for example, came in the late eighteenth century—around the time of the French and American revolutions. In his *Reflections on the Revolution in France*, as we saw in the preceding chapter, Edmund Burke attacked the Enlightenment liberalism that he saw underlying the political crisis in France. Dismayed by Burke's attack, Tom Paine picked up the gauntlet which Burke had thrown down. He wrote *The Rights of Man* in reply to the "flagrant misrepresentations which Mr. Burke's pamphlet contains."[9]

Burke and Paine differed on all kinds of issues. But one may serve well enough for purposes of illustration—namely, the problem of the ignorance of the lower orders of society. Burke and Paine both recognized that all contemporary European societies included large numbers of illiterate and "unenlightened" people. Where they diverged was in their answers to the question of what had caused this situation.

Burke's answer was not a new one. Indeed, Aristotle had expressed it centuries earlier when he wrote that some men were "slaves by nature." According to this view, men simply differ in their innate capacities. Some are born with the intelligence and will to attain wisdom and virtue. Others, because of lesser potential, simply will never become "rational" beings in the fullest sense of that word. Even if they have the ability to become truly educated and enlightened, the necessities of their station in life—their occupation—will prevent them from reaching the heights achieved by others. And this situation is both natural and unavoidable. In short, the causes of "vulgar" behavior and ignorance lie in nature and in the individual.

Accordingly, social policy which flies in the face of this natural inequality is bound to have perverse consequences. "Believe me, Sir," wrote Burke, "those who attempt to level, never equalize. In all societies, consisting of various descriptions of citizens, some description must be uppermost. The levelers, therefore, only change and pervert the natural order of things; they load the edifice of society by setting up in the air what the solidity of the structure requires to be on the ground."[10]

Paine confronted the same question quite specifically and reached a very different answer. "How then is it," he wrote, "that such vast classes of mankind as are distinguished by the appellation of the vulgar, or the ignorant, mob are so numerous in all old countries? The instant we ask ourselves this question, reflection finds an answer. They arise, as an unavoidable consequence, out of the ill construction of all old governments in Europe, England included with the rest. It is by distortedly exalting some men, that others are distortedly debased, till the whole is out of nature."[11]

In short, Paine sees society as the cause of ignorance and brutish behavior. Poor governmental arrangements produce these distorted results. And if governments were not so perversely organized, the potentialities of the common man would not be so blighted. Burke, on the other hand, sees most of this vulgar ignorance as given by nature. Society is not to blame, but instead must cope with it as best it can. And any attempts to mandate complete equality can bring only political perversion and disaster, by their refusal to respect the simple facts of human existence.

The Problem of Aggression: Pessimistic Diagnoses

Or take for another example—and an important one—the problem of aggression in social life. Where does it come from? Why do some men behave with hostility and destructiveness toward other men? Are people "naturally" aggressive? Or is aggression instead a product of "artificial" social arrangements which could be changed?

Some of the most important political theorists have taken the former, more pessimistic view. Aggression is part of human nature, they would argue. Man's natural passions and desires lead him inevitably into collision with his fellows. And when he finds these passions and desires frustrated by other men, he will respond aggressively and destructively. Governments do not create this problem; instead they confront it as a "given" with which they must cope as best they can. Indeed, one of the major functions of governments arises precisely at this point: they must uphold "law and order." They must create and enforce rules of behavior designed to prevent human aggression from degenerating into outright warfare and destroying human society.

Some theologians who ventured into political theory took this view. St. Augustine and Martin Luther, to cite two important examples, saw aggression as a product of man's natural sinfulness. Sinful man is perversely egocentric. He loves himself above all others. His own individual desires take precedence over all other considerations. Immersed in his own self-aggrandizing passions, natural man would happily tyrannize over other men. Short of genuine spiritual regeneration—the replacement of "amor sui" by "amor Dei"—man will always wish to dominate and control other men in his own behalf. The "communion of saints"—a society of the spiritually regenerate—would not need any governing power over it other than God's divine authority. But merely human societies will always require strong governments to control and contain the mutually exploitative inclinations of their members. The "City of Man" will always require forceful rulers. Or, as Luther put it with characteristic bluntness: "The world is too wicked, and does not deserve to have many wise and pious princes. Frogs need storks."[12]

Hobbes and Freud have offered very similar diagnoses of human aggression in the context of more secular and naturalistic world views. Aggression, in their view, is a natural consequence of the composition of the world and of the dynamics of the human psyche.

In Hobbes's diagnosis of the sources of human conflict, it is *nature* which "dissociates and renders men apt to invade and destroy one another."[13] Men are naturally impelled to seek power in order to fulfill their natural wants. And this power includes power over other men. Men naturally love "dominion over others."[14] Human beings desire dominion for several reasons. First, they seek power in self-defense, to prevent others from dominating them. Second, they need power in order to get worldly possessions, since there is not enough to go around to satisfy everybody. As Hobbes says, "Many men at the same time have an appetite to the same thing; which yet very often they can neither enjoy it in common nor yet divide it."[15] And third, men are naturally vain. They love glory. And not everyone can have glory, because that requires eminence over others. In the case of glory, as Hobbes writes, "if all men have it no man hath it, for it consists in comparison and precellence."[16]

Natural human passions, then, lead inexorably to political strife. Men find themselves in a zero-sum game in which contending lusts for power collide head-on. Men are not naturally peaceable social beings. They come together for gain or for glory—and both of these could be better achieved by dominion than through cooperation. The natural condition of man, in sum, is a state of war. Therefore, Hobbes writes, "men have no pleasure, (but on the contrary a great deal of grief) in keeping company, where there is no power able to over-awe them all. . . . Hereby it is manifest, that during the time men live without a common power to keep them all in awe, they are in that condition which is called war; and such a war, as is of every man, against every man."[17] Only by covenanting together to create a powerful state can men escape this "ill condition, which man by mere nature is actually placed in."[18]

Freud's diagnosis of the human condition is very similar. Man is by nature a highly aggressive animal. The *id* (his name for man's innate passions) is a "seething cauldron." Every child is a would-be tyrant who would gladly dominate or destroy anyone who prevents the immediate gratification of his desires. He is born egomaniac: "Give it to *me!*" "Look at *me*, Daddy!" When he perceives his father as a competitor for his mother's affection, he wishes him dead—the Oedipal wish. Only his natural weakness and the constraints of social forces keep him from fulfilling his inborn dictatorial ambitions.

These aggressive impulses and inclinations are only contained—either externally by superior force or by the threat of it, or internally via the control of the *superego;* they never disappear. Deep down, man always would like to dominate other men for his own pleasure, and if the circumstances permit it these desires will quickly surface—as, for example, when a conquering army rapes and pillages its victims.

In his *Civilization and Its Discontents*, Freud gave powerful expression to this bleak view of the human psyche: "Men are not gentle creatures who want to be loved, and who at the most can defend themselves if they are attacked; they are, on the contrary, creatures among whose instinctual endowments is to be reckoned a powerful share of aggressiveness. As a result, their neighbor is for them not only a potential helper or sexual object, but also someone who tempts them to satisfy their aggressiveness on him, to exploit his capacity for work without compensation, to use him sexually without his consent, to seize his possessions, to humiliate him, to cause him pain, to torture and to kill him. *Homo homini lupus.* ('Man is a wolf to man.') Who, in the face of all his experience of life and of history, will have the courage to dispute this assertion?"[19]

Faced by these powerful, potentially highly destructive human drives, "civilized society is perpetually threatened with disintegration."[20] Society must work continually and diligently to prevent the mutual hostility of its members from breaking out into physical conflict. It is no mean achievement simply for a government to be able to maintain and enforce law and order in its domain. Given man's nature, civilization is a precarious accomplishment—and occasional breakdowns of social order are almost inevitable.

In any event, Freud would argue, it is pure delusion to identify any specific set of social or governmental institutions as the source of human conflict and aggression. No diagnosis could be much further from the truth. The Marxian diagnosis that locates the source of human political strife and psychic disruption in the institution of private property, for example, is clearly faulty. Eliminating private property, attaining the classless society, may have its economic virtues or it may not. But whatever the economic consequences, these political changes will definitely not abolish the sources of human aggression. These primal instincts antedate property, and they will survive its elimination unscathed. Like all societies, a Marxist classless society can maintain a high degree of internal cohesion—through the mechanism of diverting the aggressive instincts of its members toward external enemies. But this is only a temporary expedient in the Marxist scheme of things, and a triumphant world communism would therefore only find itself faced once again with the perennial problem of civilization: dealing with individual aggressiveness. "One only wonders, with concern," Freud muses, "what the Soviets will do after they have wiped out their bourgeois."[21]

The Problem of Aggression: More Optimistic Diagnoses

On the other side of this crucial diagnostic question are equally profound political theorists who deny that human aggressiveness and destructiveness are intrinsic to man. Instead of locating the sources of human conflict, hostility, and estrangement in the "given" passions of human nature, many theorists have found these causes in the "artificial" arrangements of human society. Some of these theorists perceive human passions as basically good or convivial. Others see man as essentially devoid of truly "natural" passions and therefore as malleable by environmental forces. In either case, the root causes of social breakdown and conflict must lie, on this diagnosis, in the institutional arrangements of society. From one perspective these arrangements are viewed as perverting and distorting the naturally sociable and peaceable inclinations of men, and from the other, as shaping them poorly when they could be shaping them constructively and harmoniously.

Aristotle, for example, believed that nature is essentially ordered and harmonious. One could even call it "rational" in the sense that it is "purposeful." "That which is produced or directed by nature can never be anything disorderly: for nature is everywhere the cause of order," he wrote.[22] And this fundamental principle applies to human nature, as well.

Man, in Aristotle's view, is a creature who strives naturally toward completion and fulfillment. The human will is oriented by nature toward the good. "All men do all their acts," he believed, "with a view to achieving something which is, in their view, a good."[23] Human virtue is a product of habituation, and hence it requires good training and education. But the inculcation of virtue—and of civilized behavior—need not proceed in the teeth of natural antisocial passions, as in Freud's and Hobbes's view. "The moral virtues ... are produced in us neither by nature nor against nature"; rather, "nature prepares in us the ground for their reception."[24]

The polis is itself in accord with the natural inclinations of man, for "man is by nature an animal intended to live in a polis."[25] Therefore, although Aristotle was not blind to some of the human passions which create political problems,[26] his analysis suggested that good education and prudent institution building could create a relatively stable and harmonious society. The breakdown of social order, conversely, would not be attributable in his view so much to the eruption of man's antisocial nature as to a failure of the educational and political institutions of society.

Rousseau was an even stronger dissenter from the pessimistic diagnosis which finds the source of political disorder in nature. In his *Discourse on the Origin of Inequality*, he chooses as his epigram the passage from Aristotle's *Politics* which goes: "We should consider what is natural not in things which are depraved but in those which are rightly ordered according to nature," and then proceeds to criticize, among other views, Hobbes's diagnosis of political disorder.

Man is not naturally aggressive, Rousseau asserts. Men are born "rather wild than wicked, and more intent to guard themselves against the mischief that might be done them, than to do mischief to others."[27] A human being will instinctively defend himself, but he has no innate aggressive drives which would destroy or exploit other men and which consequently require strong controls by society. Indeed, Rousseau argues that compassion is a natural feeling in man which tempers his egoism and makes him respond sympathetically to his fellow man. Hobbes's belief in the natural enmity and mutual hostility among men, therefore, is mistaken. In fact, "nothing is more gentle than man in his primitive state."[28] Hobbes's error lay in his failure to see the compassionate side of man's nature and in ascribing to man's nature passions which in fact arise from his participation in a corrupt society.[29]

In Rousseau's diagnostic analysis, therefore, the source of human corruption is found to lie in perverse social arrangements. Nature creates men basically equal. It is the development of society which magnifies the small inequalities of nature into gross inequalities and creates and enforces new ones. "Man is born free," but "everywhere is in chains," Rousseau observes at the outset of his *Social Contract*. And while explanations of how this happened can only be conjectural, it is clear that social "artifices" are the added factors which cause the departure from natural freedom and equality.

Among these artificial institutions human beings have devised, the institution of private property is a very important source of unnatural inequality, in Rousseau's view. Property is not for him the source of all evil, as it tends to be for Marx, but it looms large in his diagnosis: "The first man who, having enclosed a piece of ground, bethought himself of saying 'This is mine,' and found people simple enough to believe him, was the real founder of civil society. From how many crimes, wars, and murders, from how many horrors and misfortunes might not any one have saved mankind, by pulling up the stakes, or filling up the ditch, and crying to his fellows: 'Beware of listening to this impostor; you are undone if you once forget that the fruits of the earth belong to us all, and the earth itself to nobody.'"[30]

The destruction of original human equality, in which the institutionalizing of property has played an important role, results in "terrible disorders," asserts Rousseau. Faced by the danger and insecurities of this new situation, which closely resembles a Hobbesian state of war (with the important diagnostic difference that Hobbes saw this as a "natural" rather than a socially created situation), men sought desperately to escape their predicament by creating a formal political society. But their escape was in fact a trap, for all but the most favored. For the new formalized society merely defended, enforced, and intensified those inequalities which had given rise to the problems in the first place. "All ran headlong to their chains, in hopes of securing their liberty; for they had just wit enough to perceive the advantages of political institutions, without experience enough to foresee the dangers." Hence, the origin of society and law "bound new fetters on the poor, and gave new powers to the rich; ... destroyed natural liberty, eternally fixed the law of property and inequality, converted clever usurpation into unalterable right, and, for the advantage of a few ambitious individuals, subjected all mankind to perpetual labor, slavery, and wretchedness."[31]

Parallel to Rousseau's criticism of Hobbes are the criticisms of Freud offered by social theorists such as Erich Fromm and Herbert Marcuse. Fromm and Marcuse do not agree on everything, but they do agree that Freud erred in his diagnosis of human aggression. Where Freud, as we noted, believed aggression to be instinctive and ineradicable in the human psyche, both Fromm and Marcuse see it as a response to social conditions that can be changed.

In Fromm's psychology, human destructiveness is not a primary drive. Instead it is a perverse form of the primary human need for "transcendence." Man, as a being endowed with reason and imagination, finds himself unable to accept the purely passive role of inanimate nature. "He is driven by the urge to transcend the role of the creature, the accidentalness and passivity of his existence, by becoming a 'creator.'"[32] Normally and properly, the need for transcendence is satisfied constructively. Man fulfills his need for transcendence by creating more life, as in raising children, or by creating works of art, by singing, loving, caring. In its normal manifestations, then, the urge for transcendence poses no threat to social order.

In fact, the propensity of men to form organized societies may be seen as partially sustained by this urge.

If the longing for transcendence is, for one reason or other, denied a normal and constructive outlet, however, it may seek different and more ominous channels of expression. Man can transcend his creaturely estate not only through creation, but also through destruction. Either way he establishes himself as a form of life which exists above the object he creates or destroys. But destructiveness and aggressiveness are not innate and primary instinctual drives in man. He does not have a given desire to destroy anything per se; he will become destructive only if there is no other way that he can express his need for transcendence. Human destructiveness is merely a "secondary potentiality" which comes into play "when the will to create cannot be satisfied."[33]

Hence in this view, as distinct from that of Freud, it is not incumbent upon society to defend itself against the instinctive aggression of the individual—or to devise ways for its "sublimation" (that is, its displacement into alternative, secondary objects). Society simply must take care to allow creative outlets for what are potentially very constructive instinctual energies. A political system need not be repressive; it need only provide opportunities for its citizens to fulfill themselves.

Marcuse's analysis is somewhat different, but he too finds Freud's account of human aggression inadequate—and politically reactionary in its implications. Marcuse proceeds by noting that Freud himself, in his later thought, saw aggressiveness as a manifestation of the "death instinct," Thanatos. But the aim of the death instinct can be seen as the cessation of tension, pain, and strife—and therefore ultimately as a negative manifestation of the pleasure principle. The only *primary* instinct in man, therefore, becomes Eros—the libidinal urge to pleasure and gratification.

As long as the world is hostile to the fulfillment of man's primary desire for pleasure and gratification—as long as the "reality principle" frustrates the satisfaction of Eros—then Eros and Thanatos, the drive toward life and the drive toward death, appear as opposite forces. But if reality can accommodate man's drive for erotic fulfillment, then the death instinct will lose its apparent autonomy and merge with Eros. In Marcuse's words, "The conflict between life and death is the more reduced, the closer life approximates the state of gratification." As repression becomes unnecessary, "Eros would, as it were, absorb the objective of the death instinct."[34]

And the fact is, Marcuse asserts, that the productive capacity of modern society has made Freud's view of the reality principle obsolete. Freud viewed reality as inevitably and eternally antithetical to man's desires for self-gratification. In the affluent society, where scarcity no longer reigns supreme, this is no longer the case, Marcuse claims. Freud's reality principle was a key component in his analysis of aggression as innate, in Marcuse's view. But Freud's concept of the reality principle reflected merely a stage of social development. It was a historical situation, not a natural and biological condition.

In modern society, Marcuse therefore concludes, repression is no longer a social necessity. If modern society constricts the free expression of the individual's desire for self-gratification, it thereby confesses its own failure. The time has come for us truly to be free; and Freud is, as it were, turned on his head. In place of the Freudian view that civilization must wage a continual struggle against its discontents, Marcuse substitutes his picture of "the unifying and gratifying power of Eros, chained and worn out in a sick civilization."[35]

These are, of course, only capsulized sketches of several highly complex and profound analyses of the human political predicament. In order to reach an adequate understanding or appreciation of them, one must turn to the original sources. However, these brief summaries do illustrate the diagnostic component of political theory, and they also provide the basis for some further observations about this stage in the dynamic logic of political thought.

Diagnostic Differences and Ideological Perspectives

It is possible at this point, for example, to identify divergent tendencies among theorists in their diagnostic conclusions. And it is possible to see how these divergent diagnoses provide a foundation for contrasting visions of the good society and for competing policy prescriptions.

The different diagnoses of the sources of human ignorance, aggression, and consequent political disorder provided by Hobbes and Rousseau, by Freud and Marcuse, by Burke and Paine implicitly contain contrasting critiques of existing political systems. To see a given society against the background of Hobbes's analysis of man's natural passions is to see it very differently from the way the same society would appear to Rousseau. Given his perception of man as naturally aggressive, Hobbes understandably saw a necessity for political authority to be strong. Given his perception of man as naturally compassionate, Rousseau understandably saw the requisites of political order very differently. Because of their underlying diagnostic interpretations, Hobbes could easily see as weak and dangerously fragmented the very same society which Rousseau would see as illegitimate and oppressive.

The same thing holds true for the other theorists we surveyed. The very same pattern of social hierarchy which Burke would see as necessary, proper, and natural would probably be seen by Paine as highly unnatural, unnecessary, and perverse. And what Freud might perceive as a society struggling desperately against the violent and disintegrative forces of the id might well be perceived by Marcuse as a repressive social order squeezing the life from the human spirit.

On the basis of our examples, then, we can distinguish what might be called conservative and radical perspectives in the diagnosis of political disorder. A political theorist who locates the causes of political disorder in *natural* forces and phenomena—that is, in the "given" order of the world—will generally be more conservative than a theorist who locates the causes of political disorder in *artificial* institutions and arrangements which men have devised themselves. Similarly, a theorist who perceives the sources of political disorder as stemming from within the *individual* psyche will generally be more conservative than a theorist who perceives *collective* malfunctions as the basic problem. A rather simplistic, but essentially accurate, depiction of the relationship would look like this:

**DIAGNOSIS OF SOURCES
OF POLITICAL DISORDER**

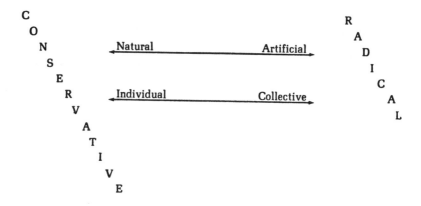

The reasons for this relationship between diagnostic position and political orientation should not be difficult to understand. For realities which are "natural," in the sense that term is used here, are by definition beyond the power of human beings to change. People can only adjust and accommodate their political order to natural "givens"; they cannot change or eliminate them, although they may be able to regulate or control them if they have the appropriate knowledge and technological capability. For example, if human aggression is the given natural attribute which Freud argues it to be, then social policy is constrained by this fact. Political programs can, and must, try to regulate the expression of human aggression so that it does not bring chaos; but no political program can do away with human aggression except by doing away with man altogether. On the other hand, if human aggression is the product of faulty political arrangements in the first place—if, for example, it arises from the institution of private property—then one could reasonably expect aggression to disappear when more salutary arrangements are devised and effected.

Similarly, a genuinely "individual" problem is one that is in some ways private and internal—and therefore not really amenable to solution by public and external means. The most perfect social program people can devise could not, for example, deliver a sinful soul from its distress. On the other hand, if personal feelings of alienation are produced in the first place by corrupt social patterns, then good political policy could provide a solution to the problem.

Our examples of the diagnostic component of political theory also help to show why political theories are often said to rest upon conceptions of man—or what is sometimes called "philosophical anthropology." As Madison wrote in a famous passage of *The Federalist Papers*: "What is government itself but the greatest of all reflections on human nature?" Any account of the good society involves an underlying set of beliefs about man—his fundamental motivations and potentialities. All of us hold such beliefs, though we may be only half conscious of them. But the political theorist, in his diagnostic inquiry, is forced to articulate rather carefully his understanding of human nature. From Plato to Marcuse, from 400 B.C. to the present, the continuing conversation of political theory has been closely intermingled with attempts to understand the dynamics of the human psyche. Attempts to unravel the causes of political disorder cannot avoid entering this area.

Other Diagnostic Issues

Not that all diagnostic issues in political theory are questions about human nature. Sometimes the crucial question is confined to identifying *which* institutional mechanism within a political system is responsible for a recognized failure. A political system is highly complex. It encompasses a large number of intertwined variables which might be causes of disorder.

Perhaps the difficulties, tensions, and ineffectiveness of a malfunctioning political system stem from an outmoded and unjust distribution of power and influence. The Marxist concept of social "contradictions" is one example of a diagnosis of this sort. No group in society, Marx observed, is inclined to give up its privileges and prerogatives, even if these have become irrational and unjustifiable. Changes in the "relations of production"—that is, in the political economy—of a system may render obsolete a political superstructure that was erected in a previous era. The tension produced by this contradiction between economic base and political superstructure then undermines the system. The tremors and convulsions in France that eventually led to the French Revolution were caused by this kind of derangement. An anachronistic feudal aristocracy refused to accommodate itself to a new social order and was eventually overthrown by force. In Marx's judgment, this pattern of contradiction and revolution was inevitable—and would be replicated in the downfall of capitalism. But one need not share Marx's beliefs in order to understand and appreciate the diagnostic perspective embodied in his analysis of social contradictions.

Or perhaps the difficulties of a disturbed political system arise from the "political culture" of the society—from the informal attitudes, beliefs, and patterns of behavior current among the members of the society. Perhaps the problem then lies in the failure of the society's educational institutions. (More than one important political theorist has become an educational reformer. Plato's *Republic* is as much a treatise on education as it is on politics. And Locke and Rousseau devoted considerable attention to education in *Thoughts Concerning Education* and *Emile*, respectively.) Perhaps the problem lies in administrative breakdowns or in unintended and unexpected by-products of basically beneficial governmental action. A myriad of institutional sources of social failure are conceivable, and the diagnoses of some political theorist or other has probably touched on most of these.

One contemporary diagnostic issue which focuses on institutional failure and which has important policy implications centers on explanations of the Great Depression. Contrasting accounts of the causes of that economic debacle are important in the contending visions of the good society offered by laissez-faire liberals and New Deal liberals. One highly influential diagnosis of the causes of the Depression was first systematically articulated by the British economist John Maynard Keynes. In his analysis, the Depression was a result of economic forces which would permit a capitalist economy to reach an equilibrium at less than full employment. His diagnosis suggests that government action may be necessary to get an economy out of a depression and to prevent future occurrences. The role of government in the economy which New Deal liberals see as proper is based in substantial part on this analysis.

A competing explanation of the Depression maintains, in contrast, that its severity and depth are attributable almost wholly to acts of commission or omission by banking authorities. If the actions of the Federal Reserve Board had been appropriate, economist Milton Friedman has argued, there would have been no depression—only a recessionary economic contraction that would have soon been overcome by the workings of the free market. If this analysis is correct, then it follows that an extensive government role in the economic sector is not only not necessary, but is likely to be counterproductive. Different diagnoses, here as in our earlier illustrations, carry different policy implications and undergird different visions of the good society.

The State of Nature as a Diagnostic Device

Understanding the nature and significance of the intellectual task we are calling the "diagnosis" of political disorder should also make it possible to understand the point of debates in some classical works of political theory about the "state of nature." Most people encountering the political treatises of Locke, Rousseau, and Hobbes for the first time often find their highly conjectural discussions about some imaginary state of nature quaintly antiquarian at best and meaningless at worst. Whatever the problems with their debates about the state of nature, however, these theorists devoted so much time and thought to them for good reason: the notion of the state of nature was an analytical device they used to aid them in the diagnostic issues they had to confront.

The attempt to envision the state of nature was a "thought-experiment," an attempt to disentangle, by a process of imaginative abstraction, the social sources of the human predicament from the natural sources. These theorists constructed a hypothetical state of nature by subtracting from existing society those features which they believed to be conventional and artificial (that is, man-made) arrangements. What was left over after this process of imaginative decomposition was then presumably those natural and eternal features of human nature which a responsible political theory would therefore have to accept as given.

Rousseau himself put it this way: Investigations into the state of nature "must not be considered as historical truths, but only as mere conditional and hypothetical reasonings, rather calculated to explain the nature of things, than to ascertain their actual origin." The intent of this hypothetical reasoning is to help man to "see himself as nature made him," to "distinguish what is fundamental in his nature from the changes and additions which his circumstances and the advances he has made have introduced to modify his primitive condition." And this determination is needed because "as long as we are ignorant of the natural man, it is in vain for us to attempt to determine either the law originally prescribed to him, or that which is best adapted to his constitution."[36]

Political theorists no longer speak of a state of nature. The philosophical assumptions which made that particular hypothetical notion seem compelling no longer carry the force they had in the seventeenth and eighteenth centuries. But the problems which that approach tried to confront still remain. Indeed, these diagnostic issues are both perennial and controversial.

They are perennial because it is often desperately difficult to decide what specific causes are most significant in producing various political disorders. Political events are so complex, shaped by so many overlapping forces, that it often is not possible to know for sure what the causes of a given problem are. When the disorder in question is historically unique or when a great number of possible causes are at work, and often both of these difficulties are present, the investigator must use some guesswork. He does not have adequate "control groups"— that is, a similar case minus one possible causal variable—to help him separate out the relative importance of the various contributing forces.

Consider, for example, the problem we surveyed earlier of deciding whether or not man is naturally aggressive. That question still is a live issue, for there are no human beings who exist wholly outside any social environment. Therefore, when men act aggressively in given circumstances, it is still possible to argue whether the behavior in question is wholly determined by environmental causes, or whether some innate potentiality or instinct is at work. We can not be wholly surprised, therefore, to find a contemporary student of animal behavior write that: "Intraspecific aggression is, in man, just as much of a spontaneous instinctive drive as in most other higher vertebrates. . . . It comes very hard to people not versed in biological thought to concede that man still does possess instincts in common with animals"; while, on the other hand a contemporary anthropologist argues that "man has virtually lost all his instincts. If there remain any residues of instincts in man, they are, possibly, the automatic reaction to a sudden loud noise, and, in the remaining instance, to a sudden withdrawal of support; for the rest, man has no instincts."[37]

These diagnostic issues are often the occasion for very lively, even bitter, controversy, a situation made possible because these questions are often not definitively answerable. And controversy becomes likely because contrasting diagnoses, as explained earlier, often tend to point in significantly different directions where policy is concerned.

Diagnostic Issues in Recent Political Controversy

Not surprisingly, then, some of the most heated academic controversies of recent years have centered around contrasting diagnoses of recognized political problems. Why did the urban riots of 1964 and 1967—Watts and Detroit—take place? A presidential task force looked into that question and concluded that the basic cause was institutionalized racism. The Watts riot, wrote the task force, "was a manifestation of a general sense of deep outrage, outrage at every aspect of the lives Negroes are forced to live, outrage at every element of the white community for forcing (or permitting) Negroes to live such lives."[38] The appropriate way to eliminate such outbreaks, then, the task force concluded, is to eliminate the ghetto itself: "The ghetto itself, with all the shameful economic, social, political, and psychological deprivation it causes, must be done away with once and for all."[39] This diagnosis was in turn challenged by social scientist Edward Banfield, who argued that these riots were not really caused by existing derangements of social institutions in general or by racism in particular. Instead, he wrote, the facts suggest "that race (and, incidentally, poverty as well) was not *the* cause of any of the Negro riots and that it had very little to do with many of the lesser ones. Indeed, it is probably not too much to say that some of the riots would have occurred even if (other things being the same) the people in the riot areas had all been white and even if they had all had incomes above the poverty line."[40] The riots, he argued, were basically "for fun and profit," growing out of the same inclinations toward "hell-raising" that have fueled many similar disturbances in widely variant times and places. In policy terms, Banfield concluded, "it is naive to think that efforts to end racial injustice and to eliminate poverty, slums, and unemployment will have an appreciable effect upon the amount of rioting that will be done in the next decade or two."[41]

These opposing diagnoses dealt with an urgent social problem, and because they pointed in such different directions, a wide-ranging controversy ensued. Similar controversies have surrounded other recent attempts to diagnose the sources of contemporary political disorders. Some "revisionist" historians have set into motion intense disputes, for example, by arguing that it was Western imperialism rather than communist aggressiveness that brought on the Cold War. Another lively debate surrounds attempts to decide whether the results, often unsatisfactory, of our educational system are caused by institutional failures or whether they are instead largely determined by biological (genetic) and environmental (social) causes over which our schools have little or no control.

Today, then, diagnoses of social ills tend to be scattered around the different social sciences. A contemporary political theorist, as a practitioner of the "master science" as Aristotle called it, would have to rely upon these inquiries and—given their lack of definitive resolution—would have to make some judgments as to which arguments are most persuasive. In earlier days, before the "knowledge explosion" and the proliferation of different social disciplines, most political theorists had to make these diagnoses more or less on their own. They did so conjecturally and on the basis of limited evidence, but they often reached insightful conclusions which still command support today.

In any case, the diagnostic component of any full-scale political theory is a crucially important one. The reader who would understand a Plato, or a Rousseau, or a Marcuse, or a Hobbes, needs to be attuned to this dimension of his inquiry. For the causal analysis which a political theorist provides in his examination of the sources of political disorder decisively shapes his prescriptive conclusions. Sound diagnoses must precede beneficial therapy.

NOTES

[1] Erich Fromm, *The Sane Society* (New York: Fawcett Publications, 1967), pp. 129-30.

[2] See, for example, Robert Tucker's *Philosophy and Myth in Karl Marx* (Cambridge, England: Cambridge University Press, 1964), esp. p. 32. Eric Voegelin holds a similar view.

[3] Ibid., pp. 239-40. (Emphasis added.)

[4] Peter Berger, "Between System and Horde," in Berger and Neuhaus, *Movement and Revolution* (Garden City, N.Y.: Doubleday Anchor Books, 1970), p. 15.

[5] Richard J. Neuhaus, "The Thorough Revolutionary," ibid., p. 96.

[6] Herbert Marcuse, *Eros and Civilization* (New York: Vintage Books, 1955), p. xvii.

[7] Op. cit.

[8] Michael P. Lerner, *The New Socialist Revolution* (New York: Delta Books, 1973), pp. 31-32.

[9] Thomas Paine, *The Rights of Man* (Garden City, N.Y.: Doubleday Anchor Books, 1973), p. 270.

[10] Edmund Burke, *Reflections on the Revolution in France*, pp. 55-56.

[11] Thomas Paine, *The Rights of Man*, pp. 295-96.

[12] Martin Luther, "Secular Authority: To What Extent It Should Be Obeyed," in William Ebenstein, *Great Political Thinkers*, 4th ed. (New York: Holt, Rinehart & Winston, 1969), p. 319.

[13] Hobbes, *Leviathan*, p. 104.

[14] Ibid., p. 139.

[15] Hobbes, *English Works*, ed. William Molesworth (London: John Bohn, 1839), vol. 2, p. 8.

[16] Ibid., vol. 2, p. 5.

[17] Hobbes, *Leviathan*, pp. 102-103.

[18] Ibid., p. 106.

[19] Sigmund Freud, *Civilization and Its Discontents*, trans. James Strachey (New York: W. W. Norton, 1962), p. 58.

[20] Ibid., p. 59.

[21] Ibid., p. 62.

[22] Aristotle, *Physics*, 8. I. 252a.

[23] Aristotle, *Politics*, I. 1. 1252a.

[24] Aristotle, *Ethics*, II, 1.

[25] Aristotle, *Politics*, I. 2. 1253a.

[26] For example: "But want is not the only cause of crimes. Men also commit them simply for the pleasure it gives them." And, "It is the nature of desire to be infinite; and the mass of men live for the satisfaction of desire." *Politics*, II. 7. 1267a and 1267b.

[27] Jean-Jacques Rousseau, "Discourse on the Origin of Inequality," in *Social Contract and Discourses*, trans. G. D. H. Cole (New York: E. P. Dutton, 1950), p. 227.

[28] Ibid., p. 242.

[29] Hobbes clearly is one of the principal targets Rousseau has in mind when he scolds those analysts who, "constantly dwelling on wants, avidity, oppression, desires, and pride, [have] transferred to the state of nature ideas which were acquired in society; so that, in speaking of the savage, they described the social man." Ibid., p. 197.

[30] Ibid., pp. 234-35.

[31] Ibid., pp. 251-52.

[32] Erich Fromm, *The Sane Society*, p. 41.

[33] Ibid., p. 42.

[34] Herbert Marcuse, *Eros and Civilization* (New York: Vintage Books, 1955), p. 215.

[35] Ibid., p. 39.

[36] Rousseau, "Discourse on the Origin of Inequality," pp. 198, 189, and 193.

[37] Cited by Fred H. Willhoite, Jr., "Ethology and the Tradition of Political Thought," *Journal of Politics*, 33 (1971), 621-22.

[38] Report of the Task Force on Assessment of the President's Committee on Law Enforcement and Administration of Justice, *Crime and Its Impact—An Assessment* (Washington, D.C.: U.S. Government Printing Office, 1967), p. 121.

[39] Ibid., p. 122.

[40] Edward Banfield, *The Unheavenly City* (Boston: Little, Brown, 1968), p. 186.

[41] Ibid., p. 205.

FOUR

ORDER AND IMAGINATION: RECONSTRUCTING THE POLIS

The perception of disorder poses another problem besides the problem of diagnosis. It raises the question of right order.

If a man experiences the political situation in which he finds himself as disordered in some way, this experience implies that some other political situation would not be disordered. Therefore, the political theorist must face the implicit question here: If this be wrong, then what is right? If this be sickness, then what is health? If this be derangement, then what is sanity? In short, the theorist must confront the question that is often taken in abbreviated accounts as *the* question of political theory: What is the good society? He must try to specify the nature of political order.

Breakdown and Reconstruction

The theorist's attempt to specify what a well-ordered society looks like proceeds in counterpoint to the particular disorder he perceives in his own society. If he has diagnosed the problem of his society as alienation, for example, then he must try to visualize what an unalienated society would be. If he sees his society as afflicted by "anomie"—a condition of social atomization and fragmentation—then he needs to explain what a nonanomic society would look like. If he sees irrationality, or insanity, or repression, he must specify what rationality, or sanity, or nonrepression would consist of. It is accurate to say, of course, that a political theorist provides us with his vision of political order. But we can better appreciate and understand his thought if we recognize that it arises out of contrast. The political theorist precipitates his image of political order out of his original apprehension of its absence or perversion.

A political theory is not immaculately conceived. It is a vision of political order painfully fashioned in contrast to the distorted political system which the theorist experiences. Not only do the anomalies, or disorders, of current politics give the theorist his *impetus* to reflection; they also provide him with the *clues* to his solution. This stage in the logic-in-use of political theory is reflected, for example, in a statement by the nineteenth-century French political theorist Henri de St. Simon: "The progress of enlightenment reveals the anomalies of the old social order, and makes the need of a new organization felt."[1]

The strains, crises, disruptions, derangements of the old order, in other words, confront the theorist with the need for an intellectual reconstruction of political order. He need not, in order to be a theorist, actually rebuild the polis. That is the task of the reformer, the man of action. But he must "rebuild" the polis in his mind. He has to provide the model of the good society. In this sense, political theories are "offered as symbolic representations of what society would be like if it could be reordered."[2]

Because his reconstruction is a vision of what society *would* be like, the political theorist must here rely to some extent upon his imagination. He is not simply providing a description of the world as it presently is. He begins there, but at this stage of his inquiry he must go on to "describe" the world as it *could be*. He looks closely at the disorders and crises of the body politic, and then imagines what it would look like if these afflictions could be overcome.

Like the George Bernard Shaw character often quoted by Robert Kennedy, the political theorist could say: "Some men see things as they are and ask 'why?' I dream things that never were and ask 'why not?'" For the political theorist is something of a visionary. He is very much concerned to see what might be. As we saw in the previous chapter, however, the political theorist must face both questions. He must reach some understanding of the "why," of the causes of the problems he perceives, if his solution is to be a rational one.

The Functions of Utopia

This vision of what could be is the utopian element of a political theory. The word "utopia" comes from the Greek *ou topos*, "no place." And this is where the ordered polis envisioned by the theorist exists—no *place*, except in his own imagination. It "exists" as a possibility. It may represent the future. It may embody a heavenly ideal. But it doesn't exist in the here and now.

Toward the end of the *Republic*, Plato makes this point. The republic is referred to by one of Socrates' young companions as "this commonwealth we have been founding in the realm of discourse; for I think it nowhere exists on earth." "No," replies Socrates, "but perhaps there is a pattern set up in the heavens for one who desires to see it and seeing it, to found one in himself."[3]

To say that the political theorist must use his imagination in the reconstructive part of his inquiry is not to say that he simply indulges himself in wild flights of fancy. He is not free to imagine whatever he pleases. His vision of political order, though "imaginary," must be firmly tied to reality. It must be a projection of real possibilities and potentialities of human life—disciplined by and grounded in the actualities of human life in society—or it will be a mere delusion.

The imaginative reconstruction of the polis produced by the theorist's utopian vision intends to be a kind of truth about the world, about politics, and about man. It is not a representation of "empirical" truth in the simple sense, of course. It is not a static and closed account of the here and now. But it is intended, nonetheless, to convey the truth about the "wholeness" or fulfillment of politics. A utopia tries to depict not what already has been done but rather what is possible for man to do and to be. It is a statement about political potentialities rather than about actuality. In the words of Paul Tillich, the concept of utopia "opens up possibilities which would have remained lost if not seen by utopian anticipation. Every utopia is an anticipation of human fulfillment, and many things anticipated in utopias have been shown to be real possibilities."[4]

Without utopian speculation, in fact, human life would stagnate. "Where no anticipating utopia opens up possibilities we find a stagnant, sterile present—we find a situation in which not only individual but also cultural realization of human possibilities is inhibited. . . . The present, for men who have no utopia, is inevitably constricting; and similarly, cultures which have no utopia remain imprisoned in the present and quickly fall back into the past, for the present can be fully alive only in tension between past and future."[5]

In turn, moreover, the theorist's vision of political possibilities tells us something about the present. Only by placing the present state of affairs against the background of its possibilities do we see our current limitations and failures for what they are. Only by acquaintance with sanity do we fully understand what it means to be neurotic or paranoid. Only by an encounter with divine grace do we fully know what it means to be a sinner. By telling us about what can be, the theorist tells us something important about what we are.

Even in his visions, his dreams, his utopian speculations, then, the political theorist takes his bearing from the facts. He is, in part, simply trying to fill in the context which justifies his original perception of disorder. To see one state of affairs as deranged implies that another arrangement would be sane—and it is incumbent upon the theorist to sketch the shape of this other, sane, situation. The political theorist draws his picture of the reconstructed polis, then, by carefully reflecting upon the specific failures which launched his inquiry in the first place.

The Dynamics of Reconstruction

The dynamics of this disciplined feat of the imagination can be explained by reference to Michael Polanyi's distinction between "tacit" and "explicit" awareness.[6] Polanyi points out that we never know anything wholly explicitly. The knowing mind always is relying upon a tacit awareness of many subsidiary features of a situation in order to focus upon that part of the situation which constitutes its explicit concern. We rely upon a background to frame the subject of our attention. We rely upon letters to attend to words, and upon words to concentrate on a meaning. We rely upon our apprehension of a person's features in order to recognize his face—without being explicitly aware of the individual features themselves. The tacit, unconscious matrix of these perceptions is in all cases essential. We can't see anything apart from some context or apart from its constituent features, even though we are not focally aware of the context or the features at the time.

Indeed, if we turned our attention to the context or to the individual features, we would lose sight of what we were trying to see. We can't read words if we attend to the letters or assimilate meaning if we look solely at the words themselves.

We can, however, shift the focus of our attention if we need to. We can look explicitly at what we had been relying upon tacitly. And in some cases, this shift of focus may be revealing or even necessary. Normally, a tennis player does not focus upon his grip—he would lose sight of the ball if he did. But he may need to attend to how he is holding the racket on occasion if a faulty grip is causing him trouble.

The imaginative reconstruction of the polis offered by a political theorist can be said to embody a systematic shift of attention of just this sort. The theorist realizes that, in order to be "seeing" part of current politics as disordered, he must be relying upon a conception of order. He may not have been aware of this conception of order at all. It very likely, in fact, played a wholly tacit role in his view of his own political situation. But he eventually is forced to recognize the crucial role which this tacit dimension plays in his critical perception of the status quo. To fill in his theory, therefore, he must turn to consider and articulate the underlying paradigm of human order which has provided him with the foundation for his vision.

To do so, the theorist inverts the original functional relationship between tacit context and explicit focus which composed his original awareness of political disorder. Instead of tacitly relying upon a conception of right order to perceive a particular political situation as somehow wrong, he now relies upon his perception of disorder as the basis for attending to his conception of right order. Instead of relying upon a tacit notion of health to recognize a disease, he now relies upon his understanding of the disease as a clue to knowing much more clearly than before what it means to be healthy. Background and foreground exchange places; though, as before, they still compose one whole picture.

Norms: Patterns of Order

The criteria of right order which the theorist articulates in his imaginative reconstruction of the polis are "norms" for political life. This is why political philosophy is sometimes referred to today as "normative theory." A norm is a shape, a pattern, a meaning, which functions as a standard. The word "norm" comes from the Latin word *norma*, originally meaning a carpenter's square. The carpenter's square, of course, is a shape or pattern which he uses as a standard. He measures the adequacy of his creations by seeing if they "shape up" to the pattern embodied in his square. And this is precisely how a theorist's normative model of politics works. It provides him with a standard by which he can judge the adequacy of existing political systems. He can use his vision of the good society as a measuring rod for seeing how his own society "shapes up."

Normative patterns appear in a variety of words and concepts. "Good" is perhaps the most general normative word, along with "right," and also the vaguest. Other normative concepts such as "justice" or "sanity" or "health" are more specific but still slippery. More technical-sounding phrases, such as "functionally integrated" or "mature," may serve normative roles as well. A normative concept, in short, is one which, directly or metaphorically, symbolizes a state of order and wholeness as opposed to disorder or incompletion.

It is important to understand that norms are not simply preferences, arbitrary expressions of individual taste. To say that a given political order is "just" is not simply to say that I "prefer" it—any more than to say that Bill is reasonably sane is to say that I "prefer" him to schizophrenic Frank. If the political theorist were simply stating his "druthers," like most of us he would probably see the ideal system as one in which he always had his own way. But that's hardly what he means by justice or the good society.

Discovery and Invention in Reconstruction

The reconstructed normative political order found in political theory is a combination of discovery and invention. It is an invention of sorts because it requires a creative effort by the theorist. The normative order which he puts forward cannot simply be "observed"; it is not an existing historical phenomenon. The political theorist must conduct a kind of "thought-experiment," conjuring up in his mind the image of a political order that realizes man's political potential.

In a way, then, the political theorist is part artist. His normative model of the good society is a kind of script for the drama of human life. It provides the plot and the roles for a political production. This aspect of political theory is what lies behind Plato's famous quarrel with the dramatic poets of his day: Plato realized that they were his rivals. In the *Republic*, therefore, he set very stringent limits upon acceptable artistic productions. And this is why in the *Laws*, another Platonic dialogue, he has his lawgiver propose this response to any dramatic poets who would request admission to his polis: "Best of strangers, we will say to them, we also according to our ability are tragic poets, and our tragedy is the best and noblest; for our whole state is an imitation [*mimesis*] of the best and noblest life, which we affirm to be indeed the very truth of tragedy. You are poets and we are poets, both makers of the same strains, rivals and antagonists in the noblest of dramas, which true law can alone perfect."[7]

At the same time, the normative reconstruction of a political theory is also a genuine discovery. It is not merely created by the theorist, but it is also found by him. In fact, the method by which he reaches his understanding of the shape of the good society has some real resemblance to the way a scientist discovers a new theory: he uses the facts of politics as the clues which lead him to the recognition of a larger pattern which "makes sense of" these facts. And, just as the scientist's discovery of a new theory may come as a virtual revelation to him, so the political theorist may feel that the light has suddenly dawned on him. Plato, for example, tried to capture the radical sense of discovery involved in the perception of right order in his "allegory of the cave." The man who discovers the truth about right order, he wrote, is like a man who has lived in a cave all his life and is then dragged up to the surface and sees light for the first time. The whole world looks different!

The reconstructive inquiry of the political theorist is a kind of discovery also because, as we said earlier, it is disciplined by objective reality. The theorist's depiction of the good society is not a private or subjective fantasy. His elaboration of a normative pattern for political life is a specification of the real potentialities of real men in the real world; he is not talking about fairies and unicorns. The reconstructive effort of the political theorist is sufficiently constrained by objective reality, in fact, for Hobbes to have called political theory "civil science."

So the reconstructed vision of the well-ordered polis produced by a political theorist is half art and half science. It is partly a work of creative invention and partly a result of disciplined discovery. It requires imagination—but imagination rooted in concrete experience. It aims at a truth, but at a truth which lies beyond the static description of the status quo.

Reconstruction: The Existential Side

The pursuit of political theory is profoundly cognitive, yet at the same time profoundly existential. The impetus toward the imaginative reconstruction of the polis is deeply rooted in the psychic structure, perhaps even in the biological makeup, of mankind. It is a task of concrete reason, not of abstract and detached speculation. It represents the intellectual side of the human organism's attempt to achieve a *modus vivendi* within its environment.

In this respect, political theory is an extremely sophisticated form of a universal task of organic life: the task of maintaining sufficient orderliness in the environment to permit the organism to function properly. All forms of life strive to maintain a balance between their internal needs and their external environment. The necessities of environmental order become more extensive and complex as life moves up the evolutionary ladder. For amoebae, protozoae, and other primitive organic forms, the demands on the environment are relatively simple: the environment must permit the satisfactory completion of locomotion, assimilation, excretion, and reproduction. By the time we reach the level of only moderately complex organisms, one essential element of a satisfactory environment becomes an orderly pattern of interaction with others of the same species. In the higher animals this need for an ordered "social" environment already produces quasi-political phenomena, as the animal seeks to maintain an orderly "objective" world.[8]

In the case of *Homo sapiens*, an important part of his environment is political. Moreover, the human capacity of self-orientation toward the world, is, in significant degree, cognitive and symbolic rather than purely instinctual. Disruption of the real or symbolic order of the political universe, therefore, brings profound stress—and distress—to its inhabitants. Because human beings cannot live in chaos, the breakdown of the meaningful order of the world causes deep consternation and demands some response. As Robert Jay Lifton writes, during times of profound social dislocation "there is always a hunger for words and acts that contribute to the re-ordering and re-symbolization of collective existence."[9]

This is exactly what the reconstructive part of political theory seeks to accomplish: to mediate between the self and the political environment, reordering a relationship which has gone awry. Prompted by political disorder and disruption, it seeks to provide the intellectual basis to "transform this disoriented civilization . . . into something a human being can identify as home."[10]

Types of Theoretical Reconstruction

It is possible to differentiate several distinctive "styles" of reconstruction in political theory. These different approaches in turn tend to match up with distinguishable styles of political action, and they can be labeled accordingly.

First, there is what could be called the "radical" approach to reordering the political world. "Radical" here does not necessarily mean "leftist," in terms of the conventional political spectrum. Rather, in the original sense of the term, it goes to the *roots*, to the very bottom, of what it perceives to be the problem. It is thoroughgoing. It often envisions sweeping changes. The radical theorist is "idealistic." He tends to be philosophical, abstract, visionary, and relentlessly "logical" in the conclusions he draws.

The radical thinker develops his vision of political order by looking closely at the failures of his polis and then conceiving a political world in which these failures would disappear. The radical sees strife or warfare and envisions a world at peace— where "the lion shall lie down with the lamb." He sees falsehood and envisions truth, sees hatred and envisions brotherhood, sees division and envisions unity, sees repression and envisions freedom.

This radical mode of theorizing may produce a wide variety of substantive theories. In fact, most epic political theorists are radical thinkers in this sense, since they probe the very fundamental questions about political order, and their reconstructed visions diverge rather dramatically from the status quo. Plato, in this respect, is just as radical in his theoretical style as Herbert Marcuse—although their visions of right order are not at all alike.

The great virtue of the radical style of theorizing is its profundity and comprehensiveness. Because they explore so deeply the bases of politics, the greatest theorists of this type retain a perennial relevance and vitality. And because these theories try to envision the full potentialities of political life, they have a lasting ability to fire the imaginations and stir the hearts of their readers.

The weakness of this style of theorizing is the opposite side of the same coin. The range of its vision may exceed its grasp. The line between visionary genius and madness is not always easy to find—and some theorists slide across it. The possibilities envisioned may prove to be impossibilities, or even sheer delusions.

Charles Fourier, for example, one of the famous "utopian socialists" of the nineteenth century, imagined a future where the planets would copulate and the oceans turn into lemonade. This kind of imagination is neither prophecy nor insight. Instead, it comes rather clearly under the heading of fantasy.

More dangerous than Fourier's rather charming lunacy are reconstructed images of political order that are less clearly demented but nevertheless unattainable. Murder and violence for the sake of "transcendental and essentially unattainable goals" are "as much a part of the West as our tradition of regard for individual destiny and worth"[11]; and the pursuit of ideals created by political theorists has been a part of this grim spectacle. Indeed, the more enticing the vision, the greater violence it might seem to justify: what are a few corpses if they are the building blocks of a new heavenly city?[12]

The "conservative" political theorist approaches his reconstructive inquiry somewhat differently. His touchstone is tradition, rather than speculative vision. The thoughtful conservative thinker does not believe that this is the "best of all possible worlds"; he is not a Dr. Pangloss. But he does tend to believe that the best guidepost for repairing contemporary political disorder is found in the collective experience of mankind. The customs and the institutions which have survived "the test of time" recommend themselves to him as an inspiration—and not as an "incubus" (as Marx believed).

The reconstructive inquiry of the conservative, therefore, is more a matter of carefully sifting the experience of mankind for images of order which retain their vitality, rather than imaginatively inferring the structure of an ideal society. The conservative believes that a sensitive and knowledgeable critical mind can see the "coherence of moral activity" in human action, and in the crunch he will appeal "from contemporary incoherence to the coherence of a whole moral tradition."[13]

The strength of the conservative theorist is his "realism." His careful grounding in the concrete experience of the past protects him against falling prey to utopian delusions. Because he relies upon the resources of tradition, the possibilities that he envisions are in fact possible. The corresponding weakness of this approach to political theory is its susceptibility to stagnation and reaction. The conservative theorist may tie his view of the possible too closely to the contingent features of the past. He may not be able to see the new possibilities—or even new necessities—that changing historical circumstances open up.

A third style of political reconstruction, falling between and overlapping with the radical and conservative styles, can be called a "pragmatic" approach. The pragmatic political man is a reformer, but a "piecemeal" reformer. His reconstructive inquiry is usually rather truncated. He is not terribly interested in pursuing the theoretical implications and foundations of his perceptions of disorder. His response is more experimental than theoretical. Better to tinker a bit with the system, he feels, rather than to think about it too much. If the wheel squeaks, oil it; don't inquire into the principles of its construction!

The political style of the pragmatist has been termed "incrementalism" or "muddling through." It is a style of thought and action which has often been observed to be a dominant pattern in this country. This approach does not produce much in the way of profound political theory, since it avoids asking ultimate questions about political order. But it is not utterly atheoretical. Norms are found and invoked, even if they are not grounded very deeply in any philosophical sense. The "un-squeaky wheel" or "what works" may be a much more superficial touchstone for political action than basic principles about order, justice, liberty, and the like; but they are norms nonetheless. Even the incrementalist must have some standards for what can count as an increment. So, while the pragmatic style produces little in the way of profound political theory, even pragmatists must engage to some extent in the task of theoretical reconstruction.

The virtues of the pragmatic style are very real. It is flexible and undogmatic. It is a style of response that avoids the danger of excessive abstraction. And it encourages consensus through compromise on specific and concrete goals, rather than causing polarization by making every issue a matter of principle.

A thoroughgoing pragmatism has its costs and dangers, though. One cost is intellectual: because they are often insufficiently theoretical and reflective, pragmatists may be largely unaware of the premises and reasons which in fact govern their actions. This lack of theoretical consciousness, moreover, can produce an incapacity for foresight. And myopia can be dangerous in politics. Rather than "muddling through," pragmatists may muddle on into a deepening quagmire. Or they may lose sight of very important basic principles. Or both. In the eyes of some critics, these weaknesses of an overly sanguine pragmatism may have played a part in the debacle of American policy in Vietnam.

Plato and the Just Polis

The reconstructive phase of political theory, then, grows out of the earlier stages of inquiry. The theorist's vision of the good society builds upon the conclusions he reached in his analysis of the nature and sources of disorder. The ordered polis which the theorist constructs "in discourse" is a reconstituted, healthy version of what he has actually *experienced* as a sick society.

This close connection of the experience of disorder with its diagnosis and the reconstructed vision is well illustrated by some of the most famous models of the good society produced by political theorists.

Take Plato's *Republic*, for example. Plato had long been a student of Athenian politics, hoping in fact to become an active political leader in his society. And in his observation of Athenian politics he had seen many problems and weaknesses. But the existential shock that pushed him into systematic reflection about political order was the trial and execution of Socrates. The starting point for his political theory, then, was the question: How could this happen?

It seemed clear to Plato that no just society could have committed such a crime. Thus, the Athenian society in which he lived, he decided, must suffer from some profound moral flaws. In particular, those who ruled the society, the political leadership, must have been corrupt. For had they been the type of men who could recognize and promote goodness in their polis, they would not have put to death their one citizen who in Plato's view best embodied human virtue.

Plato's diagnosis of the disorder of Athenian society, therefore, put heavy stress on failures of character and of education among the ruling class. "The truth is," he wrote, "that you can have a well-governed society only if you can discover for your future rulers a better way of life than being in office; then only will power be in the hands of men who are rich, not in gold, but in the wealth that brings happiness, a good and wise life. All goes wrong when, starved for lack of anything good in their own lives, men turn to public affairs hoping to snatch from thence the happiness they hunger for. They set about fighting for power, and this internecine conflict ruins them and their country."[14]

The good society, then, would have to be one which was ruled by good men. A just society must have just leaders. Only in this way, Plato decided, could a society truly be well ordered. Only when "philosophers" (a word which meant "lovers of wisdom" and not "philosophers" in the technical, contemporary sense) were kings could political societies be delivered from their ills: "Unless either philosophers become kings in their countries or those who are now called kings and rulers come to be sufficiently inspired with a genuine desire for wisdom; unless, that is to say, political power and philosophy meet together, while the many natures who now go their several ways in the one or other direction are forcibly barred from doing so, there can be no rest from troubles ... for states, nor yet, as I believe, for all mankind."[15]

The vision of the good society articulated by Plato in the *Republic* depicted a polis in which genuine philosophers would reproduce "the divine order of the world" in their souls, as Socrates had tried to do. And then, having attained knowledge of goodness and having embodied this goodness in his own character, the philosophic ruler would "mould other characters besides his own and ... shape the pattern of public and private life into conformity with his vision of the ideal."[16]

The *Republic* is devoted, therefore, to explaining the rigorous education which the philosopher-king would have to undergo and to sketching the social order which would allow him to bring society into conformity with the divine *logos*. Plato's own activities were devoted to the pursuit of this ideal. He founded a school, known as the Academy, for the training of the philosophic mind; and he always looked for a way in which his image of the good society could be brought to life.

This is, of course, but a thumbnail sketch of the detailed and provocative inquiry contained in the *Republic*. But even this sketch shows how Plato's imaginative reconstruction of political order developed from his experience and analysis of Athenian disorder. Scandalized and depressed by a corrupt society which destroyed a man who, more than any other of its citizens, embodied wisdom and goodness, Plato devised the pattern of a society which would do the opposite. Instead of persecuting its best citizens, the good society would bring them to power. Virtue and wisdom would be honored and enthroned, rather than condemned. The petty and corrupt disorder and violence of existing politics would be replaced by a replica of the divine order. And "you and we," Plato hoped, "shall find life in our commonwealth no mere dream, as it is in most existing states, where men live fighting one another about shadows and quarreling for power"[17]; instead, the polis would be the home of the good life for man.

The Founding Fathers and Ordered Liberty

James Madison, Alexander Hamilton, and John Jay faced a similar set of problems in *The Federalist Papers*. Their task was to devise a constitutional order which would not be helpless against "the instability, injustice, and confusion" which "have been the mortal diseases under which popular governments have everywhere perished."[18] Like Plato's Athens, the American colonies had suffered from what they perceived as the abuse of political power. They had, in fact, just fought a war to free themselves from the "tyranny" of George III and the British Parliament. The experience of colonial oppression stood before them as a vivid image of one form of political disorder.

On the other hand, in their reaction against the abuse of power the colonies had gone to the other extreme, constructing a governmental system too weak and fragmented to accomplish the necessary tasks of government. The impotence and disarray of the nation under the Articles of Confederation, therefore, provided the writers of *The Federalist Papers* with another image of political disorder. The reconstructed order they hoped to build had to avoid both failures: it had to avoid tyranny—the abuse of governmental power—and anarchy—the disintegration of a society suffering from the absence of governmental authority.

In confronting these political maladies, Madison took a different tack from Plato. Rather than conceiving a system in which good men would be educated and placed into power, he sought to devise a system which would thwart the attempt of ambitious and self-interested men to use the state for their own advantage. Instead of reforming character, Madison was content to refashion institutions.

In part, of course, this difference in approach was a function of Madison's unique situation. He did not have the luxury of envisioning a perfectly ideal system or of awaiting the creation of the philosophic mind. He had, instead, to recommend a constitutional framework which took men as they were rather than as they might be.

But the different visions of reconstructed political order provided by Plato and by Madison also reflected diagnostic disagreements. For Plato, the human traits of egocentricity and quarrelsomeness that threatened the polis were a corruption of human nature that could be eliminated by proper training. Madison, in contrast, believed that these human traits are "sown in the nature of man." They could be eliminated, therefore, only by eliminating liberty at the same time—and this cure would be worse than the disease: "It would not be a less folly to abolish liberty, which is essential to political life, because it nourishes faction than it would be to wish the annihilation of air, which is essential to animal life, because it imparts to fire its destructive agency."[19]

Accordingly, Madison believed that the only realistic choice was to follow a "policy of supplying, by opposite and rival interests, the defect of better motives."[20] The Platonic recourse to philosopher-kings will not do. "It is in vain to say that enlightened statesmen will be able to adjust these clashing interests and render them all subservient to the public good. Enlightened statesmen will not always be at the helm."[21] The only hope is to construct a system of mutual checks and balances, "where the constant aim is to divide and arrange the several offices in such a manner as that each may be a check on the other—that the private interest of every individual may be a sentinel over the public rights."[22]

Plato, of course, would have responded that he was the realist and Madison the deluded utopian. Only a dreamer, he believed, could imagine that institutional tinkering could save a polis filled with unjust people. He found such efforts rather pathetic, remarking of the legal reformers: "Surely there is something very amusing in the way they go on enacting their petty laws and amending them, always imagining they will find some way to put an end to fraud in business and in all those other transactions. . . . They have no idea that really they are cutting off the heads of a hydra."[23]

Both the Platonic and the Madisonian models of the good society, in short, were visions of a society capable of overcoming crucial political disasters such as each man had personally experienced. The just society depicted by Plato in *The Republic* was his vision of a polis where unity and order supplanted internal division—and where good men were honored rather than vilified. Similarly, the new political framework proposed in *The Federalist Papers* was to be a society both stable and free—delivered both from the tyranny and from the fragmentation of the authors' recent experience.

The reconstructed visions of a good society set forth by other political theorists follow the same pattern. All sorts of examples illustrate how the models of the good society created by political theorists are the healthy alter egos of the ailing societies they know firsthand. We shall mention just a few.

Thomas Hobbes and the Safe Society

Thomas Hobbes, as we saw earlier, was terrified by the prospect of political disintegration in seventeenth-century England. The bitter social divisions that divided his nation among contending sects and parties placed England, in his view, on the brink of bloody and ruinous civil war. And that collapse of political order into fratricidal violence was, for him, clearly the ultimate political disaster.

The social order which he proposed in the *Leviathan*, therefore, was devised as a remedy for these dangerous trends. The natural passions of men would inevitably drive them into a "war of all against all," in his analysis, unless a strong system of authority could be established. The state must be created and accepted, therefore, as an absolute and sovereign power. It is "that Mortal God, to which we owe under the Immortal God, our peace and defense."[24] The reconstructed model of the sovereign Leviathan, then, details the arrangements necessary for a safe, secure, and stable commonwealth which can defend and protect its citizens.

Jean-Jacques Rousseau and the Moral Community

Rousseau's focus was rather different. The corruptions of his own society seemed to him to be insincerity and inequality. French society, he believed, fostered and encouraged its citizens to repress and deny their natural human emotions and to replace them with phony and artificial social manners. At the same time it fostered and enforced excessive inequalities among its citizens. Both of these failures, in turn, led to the alienation of men from themselves and from their fellows. The moral unanimity of the polis was destroyed.

Rousseau's *Social Contract*, in response to these failures, offers the vision of a society free from divisive inequality and artificiality. All citizens in the polis of the *Social Contract* are equals. Rousseau's good society would substitute for the physical inequalities of nature "an equality that is moral and legitimate"; men would "become every one equal by convention and legal right."[25] Moreover, economic inequality would not be permitted to undermine political and moral equality—as often happened in Rousseau's France. In the political world of the

Social Contract, "no citizen shall ever be wealthy enough to buy another, and none poor enough to be forced to sell himself."[26]

In the corrupt society of his acquaintance, Rousseau complained, "we have physicists, geometricians, chemists, astronomers, poets, musicians, and painters in plenty; but we have no longer a citizen among us."[27] Moreover, "jealousy, suspicion, fear, coldness, reserve, hate, and fraud lie constantly concealed under that uniform and deceitful veil of politeness . . . of this age."[28] But in the society of the *Social Contract* men would again be true citizens, bound together in the moral unanimity of the "General Will." No longer at odds with each other because of deceit and envy, the citizens of the good society would have "only a single will which is concerned with their common preservation and general well-being. In this case, all the springs of the State are vigorous and simple and its rules clear and luminous; there are no embroilments or conflicts of interests; the common good is everywhere clearly apparent, and only good sense is needed to perceive it."[29]

In short, civil equality would replace an illegitimate hierarchy; honesty and virtue would replace deceit and fraud; unanimity would replace disunity and hostility. If Rousseau's vision were fulfilled, what he saw as the major political evils of his day would no longer afflict mankind.

Erich Fromm and the Sane Society

For Erich Fromm, the reconstructed vision is "the sane society"—a political order which would not produce in man the neuroses and "socially patterned defects" induced by current society. It would be a society "where man is the center, and where all economic and political activities are subordinated to the aims of his growth." It would be a society in which qualities like "greed, exploitativeness, possessiveness, and narcissism" would not be profitable. It is a political order that is neither simply a figment of his imagination nor an expression of his own individual preference; it is instead a sketch of a society which would accommodate and nourish "the striving for mental health, for happiness, harmony, love, productiveness" that is "inherent in every human being who is not born as a mental or moral idiot."[30]

Karl Marx: After the Revolution

One final example of the reconstructive stage of political theory is worthy of mention, not only because of its contemporary importance but also because of the interesting twist which it adds to the basic pattern. Karl Marx (and his collaborator, Friedrich Engels), like all epic political theorists, had a vision of the good society. But the Marxian reconstructed vision has some distinctive features—in form as well as in substance.

Marx was notoriously sketchy in his vision of the good society. In one famous passage he does describe communist society as a political order "where nobody has one exclusive sphere of activity but each can become accomplished in any branch he wishes" and where "society regulates the general production and thus makes it possible for me to do one thing today and another tomorrow, to hunt in the morning, fish in the afternoon, rear cattle in the evening, criticize after dinner, just as I have a mind, without ever becoming hunter, fisherman, shepherd or critic."[31] Apart from this glimmer of an idyllic economy of amateurs, however, Marx tells us very little specific about the communist society.

There was a reason for Marx's reticence on this score. He was unwilling to provide specific blueprints for the communist society because he saw himself as a scientist. He belittled those political theorists who gave detailed visions of a rational political order as "utopians"; and he derided their reconstructed visions as imaginary, however grand and enticing they might be. His "scientific socialism," in contrast to these earlier methods, he asserted, confined itself to the study of reality.

Reality, though, was not static, in his view. It has, instead, an inherent tendency to develop, to change. The pattern of this progress, evident in history, Marx characterized as "dialectical." This idea carried many implications, one of which is especially important for our present purposes. In the context of dialectical change, the *disorders* of political life are seen as "contradictions"—that is, as states of tension created by opposing forces. And dialectical change operates, Marx believed, by means of overcoming these contradictions. Indeed, one might say that the overcoming of contradictions is the motive power of historical development, in Marx's view.

Because the disorders which Marx perceived in the politics of his day were considered to be contradictions, they were therefore believed to be self-eliminating. That is to say, Marx saw the political disorders he experienced not simply as clues to what a rightly ordered society *could* be but as the source of what the more rational society of the future *would* be. The disorders of the present stage of history contained within themselves a dynamic tension that would lead to their resolution.

Marx's reconstructed vision of the good society, as a result, is put forward as a rough prediction rather than as a set of hopes. He claimed to offer an approximate description of a soon-to-be-actual social system instead of a merely possible one. His reconstructed society was a vision of the future, not of a timeless ideal.

That is why Marx's image of the communist society was hazy. It is possible to be clear and specific about one's hopes and dreams, about an abstract ideal. But, even if you know the fundamental laws of progress, as Marx believed he did, you cannot foresee the exact shape of the future. At best, you can see the basic outlines of what is to come. One of Marx's favorite analogies captures this point nicely. He could know what the more rational society of the future would look like, he said, only to the extent that he could already see it in the "womb" of present-day society. The derangements of capitalist society provided him with a negative image of socialism—but this image was only partially developed. One would fully know what the new order would look like only when the time was ripe—only when the process of historical gestation was complete and the new society was actually born. For the time being, he could tell about as much about the forthcoming communist society as one can know about what a full-grown man will look like from examining an embryo: you can see the general features but no more.

The relationship between Marx's understanding of the disorders of his own society and his vision of the rationally ordered future society, then, is an especially close one—however hazy his reconstructed vision might be. His aspirations to be resolutely "scientific," together with his understanding of the dynamics of historical change, required virtually a one-to-one correspondence between present disorder and future order.

Capitalist society was a class society; the communist society would be classless. Both the bourgeois entrepreneur and the proletarian worker were alienated; "socialist man" would be psychically integrated. Capitalist society was a world of exploitation; the communist society would be a world of mutual aid and brotherhood. Capitalist society was plagued by war; a communist world would be peaceful. The tensions and contradictions of the present, in short, would eventually become sufficiently great and intolerable that they would disappear in revolutionary upheaval. And the new order which would arise out of that upheaval would bear the same kind of resemblance to the old order as a redeemed man bears to a fallen and sinful man.

Reconstruction: Historical Setting and Perennial Relevance

This account of the nature of reconstruction in political theory, together with the examples, should help to make clear the intimate connection of this stage of inquiry with the steps that came before. The reconstructed vision of a political theorist is the luminous alter ego of the dark side of politics which he has perceived in his own experience. And the status of the reconstructed vision—its viability, its rationality, its realism—depends upon the theorist's diagnostic conclusions.

Since the specific crises of the theorist's own society are the raw materials from which he fashions his view of political order, a knowledge of what these crises were all about and the historical setting in which they took place can add considerably to a full comprehension and appreciation of the theorist in question. Understanding the political turmoil in Athenian politics around 400 B.C. provides insight into Plato's *Republic*. Understanding the peculiarities of politics in Renaissance Florence helps to explain why Machiavelli wrote about the need for a strong *Prince*. Understanding the upheavals of the Industrial Revolution are quite vital to understanding the force and meaning of Marx's *Communist Manifesto*. And so on.

At the same time, the reconstructed visions of the great political theorists are not merely historical curiosities. It is no mere accident that their inquiries have survived to be read again and again in times and places quite remote from their own. They have survived because the problems they confront lie close to the foundations of human existence. The political disorders they analyze are perennial threats to human society. The specific circumstances which demanded their attention will never reappear; but the basic general problems embodied in those circumstances may recur again and again.

The twentieth century never had to worry about Dionysius of Syracuse or about the Athenian oligarchic cabal known as "The Thirty." But the twentieth century did have to confront the tyranny of a Stalin and a Hitler, so Plato's examination of the nature and dynamics of the despotic character is remarkably applicable to modern affairs.

Political warfare between Puritan revolutionaries and Anglicans, between Levellers and absolutist monarchs, is no threat to anyone in our own time. But in 1942, an important philosopher declared the insights which Thomas Hobbes had reached by reflecting on these problems to be immediately relevant to the present. Indeed, he wrote, "it is only now, towards the middle of the twentieth century, that men here and there are for the first time becoming able to appreciate Hobbes's *Leviathan* at its true worth, as the world's greatest store of political wisdom."[32]

The mores and manners of eighteenth-century France are by now long gone, and the discriminatory categories of the three French "estates" (nobility, church, and commoners) are hardly a pressing issue in contemporary America. But the social vision produced by Rousseau in response to these realities has seemed to some "New Left" thinkers to be peculiarly relevant to their own very modern concerns. One contemporary writer of that general persuasion, seeking to illuminate the political problems of his own experience, found that "Rousseau, in particular, turned out to be a gold mine."[33]

The great political theories are perennially relevant because they come to terms with perennial problems. Civil war, tyranny, exploitation, repression, political disintegration, alienation, and abuse of power are, unfortunately, not uniquely the property of any single era. These threats to a stable, free, and productive human society are always with us—sometimes as immediate dangers, sometimes only as remote possibilities. The ideas of the political theorists who have faced these dragons before can therefore be of great value to us. And their reconstructed visions of a political life which transcends these problems can be as fresh and compelling as the day they were written.

NOTES

[1]Henri de St. Simon, "The Reorganization of the European Community," in *Social Organization, The Science of Man, and Other Writings*, ed. and trans. Felix Markham (New York: Harper Torchbooks, 1964), p. 56. Cf. also Sheldon Wolin, "Paradigms and Political Theories," in *Politics and Experience*, ed. Preston King and B.C. Parekh (Cambridge, England: Cambridge University Press, 1968), pp. 125-52.

[2]Wolin, "Paradigms and Political Theories," p. 148.

[3]Plato, *Republic*, IX, 591. As Professor Cornford observes, "heavens" does not here mean the Christian hereafter. Instead, Socrates is referring to the divine order of the cosmos which he thought was manifest in the movements of the celestial bodies.

[4]Paul Tillich, "Critique and Justification of Utopia," in *Utopias and Utopian Thought*, ed. Frank Manuel (Boston: Houghton Mifflin, 1966), p. 297.

[5]Ibid., pp. 297-98.

[6]Michael Polanyi, *The Tacit Dimension* (Garden City, N.Y.: Doubleday, 1966).

[7]Plato, *Laws*, vii, 817.

[8]Konrad Lorenz gives some examples of such behavior in *On Aggression*, translated by Marjorie Kerr Wilson (New York: Harcourt, Brace, 1966).

[9]Robert Jay Lifton, *Revolutionary Immortality* (New York: Vintage Books, 1968), p. 78.

[10]This phrase, which captures very nicely the thrust of a political theory, comes from Theodore Roszak, *The Making of a Counter-Culture* (Garden City, N.Y.: Doubleday Anchor Books, 1969), p. xiii.

11 Edmund Stillman and William Pfaff, *The Politics of Hysteria* (New York: Harper & Row, 1964), p. 13.

12 Looking back over the history of communism's pursuit of an ideal society, the Soviet writer Andrei Sinyavsky wrote these anguished lines: "So that prisons should vanish forever, we built new prisons. So that all frontiers should fall, we surrounded ourselves with a Chinese wall. So that work should become a rest and a pleasure, we reintroduced forced labor. So that not one drop of blood be shed any more, we killed and killed and killed." *On Socialist Realism* (New York: Pantheon Books, 1960), p. 38.

13 Michael Oakeshott, *Rationalism in Politics* (New York: Basic Books, 1962), p. 106.

14 Plato, *Republic*, vii, 521.

15 Ibid., v, 473.

16 Ibid., vi, 500.

17 Ibid., vii, 520.

18 James Madison, *The Federalist #10*, in *The Federalist Papers* (New York: Mentor Books, 1961), p. 77.

19 Ibid., p. 78.

20 Madison, *Federalist Paper #51*, in ibid., p. 322.

21 *Federalist Paper #10*, in ibid., p. 80.

22 *Federalist Paper #51*, in ibid., p. 322.

23 Plato, *Republic*, iv, 427.

24 Hobbes, *Leviathan*, p. 143.

25 Rousseau, *Social Contract*, p. 22.

26 Ibid., p. 50.

27 Rousseau, "Discourse on the Arts and Sciences," in *Social Contract and Discourses*, p. 169.

28 Ibid., p. 149.

29 *Social Contract*, p. 102.

30 Fromm, *The Sane Society*, pp. 241-42.

31 Karl Marx, "The German Ideology," in *The Marx-Engels Reader*, ed. Robert C. Tucker (New York: Norton, 1972), p. 124.

32 R. G. Collingwood, *The New Leviathan* (Oxford: Clarendon Press, 1942), p. iv.

33 Marshall Berman, *The Politics of Authenticity* (New York: Atheneum, 1970), p. xii.

FIVE

PRESCRIPTION

Modern philosophers have made a great deal of the "logical gap" between *is* and *ought*. As these philosophers insist, a conclusion in the imperative mode—"You *ought* to do this!"—cannot be derived logically from premises which are entirely indicative—"This *is* the case." All of the "is" statements in the world cannot add up, deductively, to a prescriptive conclusion.

David Hume gave classic expression to this distinction between is and ought in his *Treatise of Human Nature*. "In every system of morality, which I have hitherto met with," he wrote, "I have always remarked, that the author proceeds for some time in the ordinary way of reasoning, and establishes the being of a God, or makes observations concerning human affairs; when of a sudden I am surprised to find, that instead of the usual copulations of propositions, *is*, and *is not*, I meet with no proposition that is not connected with an *ought*, or *ought not*. This change is imperceptible; but is, however, of the last consequence. For as this *ought*, or *ought not*, expresses some new relation or affirmation, 'tis necessary that it should be observed and explained; and at the same time that a reason should be given, for what seems altogether inconceivable, how this new relation can be a deduction from others, which are entirely different from it."[1]

The Prescriptive Penumbra of Facts

In the narrow logical sense, of course, Hume's observation is unexceptionable. One cannot *deduce* an ought from an is. Yet to leave the matter there can be severely misleading. The gap between is and ought seems to make a mystery of one of the commonest facts of everyday life—namely, the profound bearing of claims about how the world *is* on what men *do*. We all guide our actions by our understanding of reality. And we all respond quite readily to questions about why we did something by pointing to facts about the world.

Only madmen moralize in a vacuum. We rightly expect other men to be able to give us *reasons* for imperatives which they address to us. And these reasons rely upon facts. "Get off the railroad tracks!" "Why?" "Because a train is coming." The descriptive grounding in the facts of life gives any imperative its force and meaning. Without this factual grounding, the imperative becomes empty and irrational. "Get off the railroad tracks!" "Why?" "Because I want you to." "So what?" Only in worlds such as those created by Lewis Carroll or Franz Kafka do prescriptions stand alone. In the real world in which we live, if it is at all sane, prescriptive recommendations require factual grounding.

Even the simplest statement of fact carries a prescriptive penumbra. If you tell someone, "That is a chair," you could be said to be implying that the object in question is something on which to sit. And you also might be said to be implying that he ought not try to cook with it or pray to it. These are not, however, strictly logical implications. One cannot deduce them from your factual statement. But, in a less restricted sense, these inferences for action can clearly be deemed "logical." They are part of what it means for something to be a chair. You are not logically (that is, deductively) required to sit on it, but that is clearly its appropriate function.

Statements of fact, in short, carry prescriptive "implications" in the loose sense because they determine the limits of *fitting* and *appropriate* responses. A man who varnishes his dog and pats his table is not committing an error of logic, but one would feel inclined to say that he has made a mistake, nonetheless. And if, when you pointed out to him what he had done, he insisted that he had intended to do precisely that, then you still could not charge him with faulty logic; but you would surely think him a bit weird.

The more profound and the more comprehensive a description is, the more profound and compelling will be the "prescriptive implications" that it generates. A comprehensive vision of the world will not be expressed in imperative syntax—through orders, demands, and exhortations—but it will exert a tremendous influence upon the behavior of a normal man who is convinced of its truthfulness. And this is precisely how a political theory, with its profoundly comprehensive vision of political order, has important prescriptive consequences. By shaping our view of what the world of politics is all about, it inevitably will shape our political actions as well. The "prescriptive" parts of political theory, then, are inferences for fitting, proper, sane, "rational" responses to a world which is seen to be structured in a particular way.

A comprehensive vision of reality does not by itself logically generate definitive prescriptions, but it clearly and dramatically circumscribes what can count as "reasonable" behavior. As Theodore Roszak has written, "Our action gives voice to our total vision of life—of the self and its proper place in the nature of things. For most of us," he continues, "this world view may elude the grasp of words; it may be something we never directly attend to. It may remain the purely subliminal sense of our condition that spontaneously forms our own perceptions and our motivations. Even before our world view guides us to discriminate between good and evil, it disposes us to discriminate between real and unreal, true and false, meaningful and meaningless. Before we act in the world, we must conceive of a world; it must be there before us, a sensible pattern to which we adapt our conduct."[2]

Linkages Between Is and Ought

The mysterious missing links between "is" and "ought," between descriptions of the world and prescriptions for action, therefore, turn out to be neither missing nor mysterious. One of these links is the *reality principle*. The other is the force of *natural human impulse*.

The reality principle simply enjoins us to act "realistically." It counsels us to base our actions upon a clear-sighted perception of the world as it really is—and not as we might like or imagine it to be. Action that is governed by the reality principle must separate out dreams and delusions from genuine realities and possibilities. It cannot be based on the belief that the moon is made of green cheese or that there is a pot of gold at the end of the rainbow.

The force of natural human impulse is simply the consequence of "normal" behavior patterns in men. *Logically*, men could seek out chaos, pain, tyranny, and self-destruction. But *normally*, men will seek to avoid these perils in favor of order, happiness, liberty, and fulfillment. Accordingly, if you say to someone that this road leads to fulfillment, that road to destruction, you are saying nothing prescriptive in the strict sense. You are not saying that he *ought* to take this road instead of that road. But he almost surely will do so, if he believes you, because he ought to do so *if* he prefers fulfillment to destruction—if, that is, he is normal and sane.

It is not essential, given the fact of our normal inclinations as human beings, for the political theorist to speak prescriptively for his words to have prescriptive impact. That is to say, he need not use imperative terms in order for his reader to draw prescriptive inferences from his vision of politics. He need only "tell it like it is." The natural proclivities of his audience will do the rest.

In a way, political theories are like those old mariner's maps whose borders contained the admonition "Here be monsters!" or which showed a dropping-off point at the ends of a flat world. These maps didn't need to say "Keep out!" or "Stay away!" Only a suicidal sailor would fail to draw that conclusion.

Regarding the impact of his own political theory, Hobbes was quite clear about this pattern. Men fall into turmoil and civil war, he wrote, not because they want to, but because they "know not the causes of war nor peace."[3] If they are led to understand the nature of "politique bodies"—that is, to understand his political theory—then they will act to build a strong, authoritarian state to deliver them from danger. No one will need to command them or cajole them: instructing them in the science of politics will do the job quite well, owing to the influence of natural human passions. For, in Hobbes's words, "All men, as soon as they arrive to understanding of this hateful condition, do desire, even nature itself compelling them, to be freed from this misery."[4]

Now Hobbes, it is safe to say, had his peculiarities. More so than most philosophers he saw an intimate connection—perhaps even an identity—between what men *would* do out of self-interest and what they *should* do in the interest of the whole society. So he may state the case for the connection of is and ought via the force of natural human impulse too strongly.

At the same time, however, it seems to be pretty clear that if you understand the political world the way Hobbes does, you probably would draw similar conclusions about what makes a fitting and proper response to the situation. In any case, the "rational" options are severely circumscribed by his vision of reality.

Similarly, if you understand politics in the way Burke does you are probably going to be conservative politically. If you understand politics in the way Locke does, you will undoubtedly be liberal in many fundamental ways. And if you understand the world of politics as Marx does, you will almost surely bend your efforts toward the attainment of a classless society. (In fact, the historical record in this respect stands as something of an ironic reproach to Marx's own insistence on the class-bound character of political allegiance. The leadership of Marxist movements has generally come not from the spontaneous action of proletarians, driven by class interest, but rather from bourgeois intellectuals, driven by the force of Marx's vision.) In each case, the pattern of the comprehensive vision carries implications for actions which would be both realistic and sane.

If the world is what some political theorist (or philosopher or ordinary man) says it is, then some patterns of behavior have to be seen as *anomalous*. That is, some human actions—perhaps some very widespread human actions—will be seen as radically inappropriate responses to the human predicament. It is not so much that certain acts are "wrong" in the narrow and moralistic sense of that word, as that these acts are not fitting and proper in the context. They are wrong in the sense that it would be wrong for someone to smile happily when told that his child had been run over by a car, or for someone to hit you when you greeted him. In cases like that you would assume either that the individual in question didn't understand what had been said or that he was a peculiarly perverse character.

If political societies are in fact, as Burke insists, profoundly organic in structure, then it would be a mistake to treat them as if they were like mechanical artifacts. If men are communal creatures bound to their societies by tradition and emotion, as he also insists, then it would be a mistake to treat them like rationally self-interested individualists.

In the same fashion, if justice is in fact the virtue of the soul, as Plato contends, and if justice is what he sees it to be, then Napoleonic quests for power are simply absurdly inappropriate responses to the human condition. Any man seeking happiness and fulfillment should prefer being the weakest philosopher to being the strongest and richest tyrant in the world. For the just man is, in the long run, the only happy man. And the tyrant, Plato argues, not only destroys other men but will inevitably destroy himself. He will be consumed by his own insatiable hunger for power—if others do not kill him first. It is the despotic man's "inevitable fate either to be destroyed by his enemies or to seize absolute power and be transformed from a human being into a wolf."[5]

Likewise, if one comes to see the world through Marxist eyes, it becomes irrational to support the capitalist system. If Marx is right about the nature and structure of politics in bourgeois society, only someone who is unrealistic or abnormal could lend it his support. Only the sadistic or self-destructive could be pleased by alienation or exploitation—and Marx insists that these are the inevitable outcomes of capitalist society. Of course, a wealthy capitalist might decide that Marx was right and still be reactionary out of short-run self-interest. But adopting this response would have substantial emotional costs: our hypothetical capitalist would have to live with a none too favorable self-image. He would have to see himself as an exploiter and a "commodity-fetishist"; and few men can tolerate that much tension between their beliefs and their actions.

The gap between is and ought narrows considerably, then,

because the ought is never completely arbitrary. Men with normal motivations and sympathies will feel bound to respond in certain ways to certain realities. A normal man who inhabits a Burkean world will not be "bound" to respond to political events in the same way as a man who inhabits a Marxian world.

The Complexity of the Facts

If the ought is not so arbitrary as Hume implied, moreover, the is is not so clear and simple. Full-scale visions of political order escape proof. They always require an element of judgment. It may not be hard to determine some simple and isolated facts of politics—for instance, that there are 100 members of the U.S. Senate. But it is devilishly difficult to know, comprehensively, what politics is all about.

A fully comprehensive picture of what is—especially in the realm of politics—must include assessments of *potentiality*, of *possibility*, of *necessity*, and of *reality*. Each of these dimensions of what is true about the world has a significant bearing on what can count as rational political action. Each of these dimensions plays an important role in political theory. And none of them is subject to simple proof, although evidence can clearly be offered in support of specific claims about the possible, the real, and the necessary.

We can know that something is possible if it is already achieved—but then its possibility is no longer an issue. If it has not been achieved it may be highly debatable whether it is an impossibility or whether it simply has never been tried. Some say that Christianity has been tried and found wanting; others maintain that it has never been tried; still others declare that it could never be tried. Some say a classless society would solve our social problems; others contend that, whatever its alleged virtues, its achievement is an impossibility.

We can know, regarding necessity, that *a* and *b* have always been associated. But, as Hume also pointed out, that only means that *a* and *b* have constantly been conjoined, not that they are related by necessity. We cannot "observe" causes;

we must impute them. So, for example, we may find that within our own experience strong governments have always been present whenever law and order prevailed in a society; but we do not know for sure that the two *necessarily* go together.

And while we may feel fairly sure that we can discriminate between things that are real and mere dreams, fantasies, or mirages, we can never be sure. Dreams seem real at the time, as do mirages to men with parched throats in the desert who crawl desperately toward the "water" just ahead.

The prescriptive impact of these difficult judgments about what is the case—about what is possible, necessary, real— should be readily apparent. In the first place, as is often said, "ought implies can." You would rightly consider someone who ordered you to fly out of an open window to be quite mad. No one can rationally demand the impossible. Similarly, no one can contravene the necessary. If someone told a waiter, "Bring me a Tom Collins, but without gin," the waiter would be left in a quandary. And sound policy always requires a distinction between realities and mere appearances: "Don't walk out on the ice! It looks solid, but it's actually quite thin."

Many of the most famous and most important battles over policy prescriptions in political theory have turned on just these kinds of difficult "factual" determinations.

The Horizon of Potentiality

Consider first the problem of human potentialities. What people are *potentially*, what they *can* be in their fulfillment, is a question about reality—about "human nature." It is not merely a subjectivistic fancy or preference. But, as we saw earlier, it is not easy to judge, and it is impossible to prove definitively, what human nature really is. And whether a given policy prescription is "rational" or not—whether it is an appropriate response to the realities of the situation—often hinges directly on the answer to this question.

Are all people potentially happy, loving, kind, and communal creatures? If so, the many who are unhappy, unloving, and unsociable must have been thwarted from reaching their innate potential by their social environment—by their political institutions. It would therefore seem entirely fitting and proper, even obligatory, for any concerned person to work toward the transformation or the outright destruction of these life-blighting political structures.

Or are human beings, on the contrary, potentially murderers, rapists, and tyrants? If so, the record of existent political structures looks much better. They have not brought universal peace and freedom, but they haven't had much to work with. If anything, they have succeeded remarkably, given these dark proclivities of human nature, in preventing people from destroying one another. Prescriptively, it becomes more appropriate to bolster the forces of "law and order" rather than to tear them down.

Depending on the contextual backdrop provided by one's view of human potentiality, the same political institution can be seen as a rock of stability or as an obstacle to development. And the prescriptive implications which recommend themselves to people of good will must then vary accordingly.

The Limits of Possibility

Beliefs about human potentiality are often linked to judgments about what is *possible* politically. And an accurate assessment of the horizon of possibility in politics is obviously crucial to making sound political prescriptions. One good example of a theoretical clash in this category that has clear prescriptive impact is the collision between Freud and Marx over the possibility of a classless society. For Marx, such a society is not only possible; it is inevitable. The human potentiality for a wholly peaceful, free, and just society *will* be realized by history. One can choose either to get on the historical bandwagon or to get run down by it. The former choice is clearly the only "rational" option—especially since the dynamics of history are not only irresistible but rational and humanly liberating. Freud sees the whole thing very differently. His understanding of human nature consigns the Marxian dream of the final communist society to the realm of delusive fantasy. He feels that men simply are not constituted in a way that makes the realization of this utopian vision possible; man's ineradicable aggressiveness, possessiveness, and egocentricity won't allow it. Prescriptively, then, Freud undercuts completely the rationality of Marxist politics. For if he is accurate in his assessment of human potentiality, the pursuit of the ideal communist society is like chasing a will-o'-the-wisp. One simply cannot reach the desired goal. It is impossible. And the attempt to force history into a mold produced by such a fantasy can clearly have disastrous results.

Centuries earlier, Aristotle criticized Plato's vision of a unified communal society on very similar grounds. Despite the philosophical gulf which separates him from Marx, Plato also prescribed the creation of a communist society—among the guardian class, at least. The "guardians," the philosophical ruling elite, were to be denied private property in order to prevent discord among them. But, in Aristotle's view, the political ideal set forth in The Republic was simply not a genuine possibility. Plato erred, he believed (just as Freud believed Marx erred) in ascribing the evils of political division to the institution of private property. "None of these evils," wrote Aristotle, "is due to the absence of communism. They all arise from the wickedness of human nature."[6]

Partly because of this diagnostic error, then, Plato had put forward an impossible political ideal. Plato's ideal polis could never exist, Aristotle argued, for it would not, in fact, be a unified and coherent society at all. Given the realities of human nature, Aristotle contended, that would be an impossibility. Instead, this allegedly ideal polis either: 1) would possess all the evils of the old polis, 2) would never be accepted by the citizens who were not guardians, or 3) would "inevitably be two states in one, and those two states will be opposed to one another—the guardians being made into something of the nature of an army of occupation, and the farmers, artisans, and others being given the position of ordinary civilians."[7]

On the other side of the same coin, it may be important to establish the possibility of political arrangements or accomplishments which had previously been believed unattainable. Locke's Letter Concerning Toleration, for example, is largely devoted to an argument of this sort. Locke wanted to demonstrate that separation of church and state was a possible means of institutionalizing the religious pluralism that followed the Reformation. Warring among the different Protestant denominations, each of whom wanted to control the state apparatus to avoid political persecution, posed a grave threat to England. Since it was generally assumed that a viable polity had to rest upon, or at least correspond to, a commonly established religion, Locke's proposed solution had received scant consideration. What Locke was able to demonstrate to the satisfaction of his contemporaries was that toleration and church-state separation could work. It would be possible to distinguish the jurisdiction of political and religious bodies without harming the legitimate tasks of either.

In a similar way, Herbert Marcuse's argument in *Eros and Civilization* tries to establish a new political possibility. The general assumption, made explicit by Freud, had been that civilization depended to some extent upon repression—that is, upon forcing individuals to renounce or forgo some of their instinctual desires In this view, it is simply not possible for any society to give free rein to all its citizens, since their incompatible and unattainable wishes, if pursued without restraint, would tear the society apart. Marcuse tries to argue, on the contrary, that the gratification of the individual's libidinal desires is now possible The new economic plateau reached by industrial society could permit it to be wholly nonrepressive. Full instinctual gratification, then, is compatible with an ordered society. Marcuse's claim, it seems safe to say, is quite important if it is true. It is also safe to say that his claim has left many unconvinced.

The Constraints of Necessity

The prescriptive aspects of a political theory may often be rooted in judgments about what is *necessary* or *inevitable*. Just as it is absurd to demand what is not possible, it is equally irrational to demand the abolition of the necessary. Both demands are clearly delusionary. Political prescriptions, to be at all realistic and hence compelling, must respect the limitations set by the world upon human contrivance.

The language of necessity, of course, is often ambiguous. Sometimes we say that something *must* happen when we simply *want* to see it happen. The compulsion involved is our own intense desire. Political theorists are not immune from this tendency. They, too, may use the language of necessity to convey their own strong preference for a particular policy. But there is often much more to it than that. Some of the more important prescriptive recommendations of political theorists rest upon their perception that the world "objectively" necessitates certain actions. Or, somewhat more precisely, their prescriptions involve the claim that a satisfactory political strategy must reckon with certain necessary and unavoidable facts of life. Pure logic, in the narrow sense, does not foreclose fighting the inevitable. Ought is not here deduced from is. It is simply that such actions are futile.

One form of the argument from necessity imputes a determined and unavoidable course to political events. These are the doctrines of historical determinism, or historical inevitability. Marx, and his predecessor Hegel, are the foremost examples of important political theorists whose prescriptions receive their force from this kind of doctrine. In their view, history contains its own internal dynamics which will inevitably shape the future. This internal logic of history is destined to prevail over any efforts which mere mortals may exert to the contrary. The choice confronting man, therefore, becomes narrowed to a fairly stark alternative: either ride with history or be crushed by it.

Despite his condemnation of the bourgeoisie, therefore, Marx insisted that he was not a moralist. Undoubtedly Marx underestimated the role that his moral passions played in his denunciation of his opponents. But what he intended to convey by his insistence that he was a scientist rather than a moralist was the recognition that his prescriptions were determined by the alleged necessities of the world. He contended that the defenders of bourgeois society were "wrong." But they were not so much "morally" wrong, he felt, as they were "scientifically" mistaken. He judged their actions to be wrong in the sense that they were profoundly anomalous to, out of synchronization with, the inevitable progress of history.

Appropriate political policies also have to contend with what might be termed the *sociologically inevitable*. If the nature of human society is such that it unavoidably includes certain features or conditions which are essential to its existence, then anyone presuming to offer recommendations must take this into account. It would run counter to the whole purpose of a doctor's prescription for it to contain advice directed toward the demise of his patient. Reasonable counsel for a society, therefore, has to respect any necessities which are intrinsic to the society.

Many of the most significant prescriptive recommendations of political theory are calculated to respond to alleged necessities of this sort. Sociological necessity is specifically appealed to by political theorists as a principle of disqualification. That is, reference to the socially necessary or inevitable serves to disqualify the claims of opposing political theories. One's own theory is not exhaustively justified by citing the necessity in question, but key contending views are eliminated, leaving the theorist's own position unscathed. His own theory, then, emerges as the only alternative, or perhaps as one of a very few existing alternatives, which is sufficiently realistic—by virtue of its appreciation of these inescapable necessities.

Edmund Burke, for example, made considerable use of this form of argument in his criticism of the egalitarian liberalism of the French revolutionaries. His conservatism, he argued, was based in substantial part upon a clear perception of some of the necessary features of all human society—features apparently ignored by his adversaries. The revolutionaries' insistence upon total equality, Burke contended, simply flew in the face of reality. Society of necessity includes different categories of individuals, distinguished by their social role and function. And these different categories of people could never be entirely equal. "Believe me, Sir," he inveighed, "those who attempt to level, never equalize." For, "in all societies, consisting of various descriptions of citizens, some description *must* be uppermost." (Italics mine.) Those who ignore this necessity, therefore, "only change and pervert the natural order of things."

They think they are "combating prejudice," but they are "at war with nature."[8]

In similar fashion, Burke argued, the liberals' insistence on individual liberty and natural rights was also unrealistic. These libertarian demands ignored the fact that society *necessarily* constrains and thwarts some of the desires of its members. That is why society was created in the first place: to deliver men from the destructive freedom of an unsocialized condition. "Society requires not only that the passions of individuals should be subjected, but that even in the mass and body, as well as in the individuals, the inclinations of men should frequently be thwarted, their will controlled, and their passions brought into subjection." Moreover, Burke argued, with obvious implications as to the feasibility of fully representative government: "This can only be done by a power out of themselves, and not, in the exercise of its function, subject to that will and to those passions which it is its office to bridle and subdue."[9] (Italics mine.)

Hobbes offers the same kind of argument from necessity on behalf of a united sovereign power. The ultimate authority in any society, he maintained, must be located in a single place. Otherwise, the society cannot last. Attempts to divide sovereignty in a state—to institutionalize a separation of powers, for example—necessarily lead to its downfall. "For what is it to divide the power of a commonwealth, but to dissolve it; for powers mutually divided destroy each other."[10] Montesquieu and Madison, on the other hand, leading exponents of a separation of powers, argue that this "ain't necessarily so."

Positive prescriptions in this vein—that is, arguments that a particular action is necessary—are theories of contingent necessity. In other words, these arguments assert that *if* a certain goal is to be attained, *then* a specific policy becomes necessary. The recommended policy is claimed to be a *necessary means* to a generally desired end. These prescriptive arguments tend to be closely intertwined, then, with the causal analyses found at the diagnostic stage of inquiry.

Burke, again, provides us with suggestive examples. The French revolutionaries wished to destroy the hold of tradition on the minds of the people, while encouraging their devotion to posterity. But Burke argues that this approach eliminates one of the necessary means to the desired end. "People will not look forward to posterity," he writes, "who never look backward to their ancestors."[11] If you want to encourage a citizenry to look forward to the welfare of their descendents, in other words, Burke claims, you must also encourage a respect for the legacy of the past.

Similarly, Burke's adversaries intended to build a society which was both free and equal. They wished at the same time to abolish all class distinctions and to guarantee individual liberty. But Burke argues that the one policy necessarily subverts the other. A certain amount of class distinction, he claims, "composes a strong barrier against the excesses of despotism, as well as it is the necessary means of giving effect and permanence to a republic. For want of something of this kind, if the present project of a republic should fail, all securities to a moderated freedom fail along with it; all the indirect restraints which mitigate despotism are removed."[12]

The crux of James Madison's argument in *The Federalist* also is a claim about necessary means to the end of liberty. In his view, the key institutional arrangement which serves as a bulwark of freedom is not class differentiation but is, instead, the very same pattern which Hobbes decried as subversive of social stability—namely, the separation of powers. "The preservation of liberty," Madison writes, "*requires* that the three great departments of power should be separate and distinct."[13] If Madison is correct, only someone willing to abandon the cause of liberty can oppose the constitutional pattern he is advocating.

Sometimes political theorists allege or imply certain actions to be necessary without directly specifying the end. This omission could be seen as fatal to their argument. And it is part of the grounds for some critics' relegating the prescriptions to the status of mere "preference." For if someone claims a particular action to be necessary (but not inevitable) and he doesn't say necessary *for what*, then his argument seems to hang in a vacuum.

What is often involved here, however, is an inarticulate major premise which is held to be compelling almost by definition—and hence not to require spelling out. For example, this tacit major premise may be "If you wish to live in order rather than in chaos ...," which can be assumed, since men cannot live in permanent chaos. Or the unstated premise often is simply "If you wish to be human ... " Logically, of course, no one is compelled to accept this premise. But it can be assumed that the theorist's reader will naturally accept it almost by definition. The only alternatives to existence as a human being are to be a beast, which is not desirable; to be a god, which is not possible; or to be suicidal, which is not likely.

In its most primitive form, the "if you are to be human, then you must ... " argument refers simply to the necessities of physical survival. Hobbes, for example, saw his political theory as embodying the necessary means to "being human" in this very basic sense. Nature, he believed, "dissociates and renders men apt to invade and destroy one another."[14] It is possible for men to escape from this "hateful condition," but in order to do so they must covenant their submission to a rather absolutist political regime. Hobbes devotes much of his political theory to demonstrating this alleged necessity. And if he is successful in doing so, he feels, men will certainly pursue the means he sets out—because they naturally are impelled to avoid the alternative of violent death. The end of self-preservation, in short, can be taken for granted as compelling.

For most political theorists, moreover, "being human" means more than simple survival. People may be able to exist physically in situations which nevertheless do not allow them truly to "be human" in a deeper and fuller sense. Certain policies or institutions, therefore, may be recommended on the grounds that they are humanly necessary. They are requisite to existence as a moral being or to the actualization of human nature. The basic situation of being a member of a society, for example, may be seen as essential to being human. This is what Aristotle meant by saying that man was a "political animal." The man who is isolated, he contended, "who is unable to share in the benefits of political association, or has no need to share because he is already self-sufficient—is no part of the polis, and must therefore be either a beast or a god."[15]

Other political arrangements may be condemned on the

grounds that they are incompatible with the essential conditions of human life. Many political theorists have argued, for instance, that any position of absolute dependency is unacceptable for this reason. A truly human being must have a measure of autonomy. "To renounce liberty is to renounce being a man," says Rousseau in his *Social Contract*; "such a renunciation is incompatible with human nature."[16] And Plato argues that the opposite political status from total dependence—namely, the holding of complete power over others—is also incompatible with being genuinely human. The despot is placed in a situation which destroys his humanity and turns him into a "wolf."

If Rousseau and Plato are to be believed, then, the requirements of human nature prohibit certain political arrangements, just as they legitimate others. *If* you are to be human, you *must* be neither slave nor despot. If you don't wish to be human, of course, their arguments are no longer at least prima facie compelling. But they are entitled to make that assumption as a reasonable supposition. For if you don't want to be human, what do you want? Indeed, what else, realistically, can you want to be?

Realities and Illusions

Political theories also generate important prescriptive recommendations from the *reality-judgments* they contain. If necessity is the floor of a genuinely habitable human society, and possibility the ceiling, its walls are the bounds of reality.

At the level of simple, brute facts, it may not be too difficult to distinguish the real from the unreal. "There are four apples here." "That costs five dollars." We can usually judge the truth or falsity of statements like these without a great deal of difficulty.

As our vision of the world rises to higher and higher levels of complexity and comprehensiveness, however, things get progressively more difficult. At more comprehensive levels of vision the individual "facts" acquire their shape and meaning from their relationship to the encompassing whole. The surrounding context gives the constituent elements their identity.

"Is that a star or a planet up there?" Only someone with a certain theoretical sophistication can comprehend this question, much less provide an answer.

Distinguishing the real from the unreal in human affairs can be especially difficult, since the contextual background is so complex and extensive. Our understanding and, because we are men ourselves, our normal responses, will shift with our changing apprehension of this context. It is one thing to see a man hitting a small child. It is another, although the "observation" involved may be exactly the same, to see a father spanking his son. And at an even higher interpretive level, it is one thing to see this act as a process of "chastening the soul" and another to see it as "repressing the psyche." The last two phrases, as much as the simplest phrase "hitting a child," aim to be "empirical"— to describe reality. They involve, however, a great deal more interpretation (that is, they rely upon a more complex theoretical framework). And they are correspondingly more difficult claims to adjudicate.

Even at the simplest level, of course, our perceptions of reality may be flawed and mistaken. "That stick in the water is crooked"—no, that is an optical illusion. "There's water on the road ahead"—no, that is a mirage. At the higher levels of perception, where things get more and more complex, the possibility for mistakes of this sort increases geometrically. At these levels, it may be very difficult indeed to determine what is "really real." At best, some sophisticated judgments come into play. And all political theories, which try to offer a very comprehensive vision of a very complex form of life, contain judgments of this sort.

Our language abounds in terms which refer to mistaken judgments about what is real. We speak of dreams and fantasies, chimeras and mirages, illusions and delusions, superstitions, myths, and figments of the imagination. We know that it is often easy to fall prey to these maladies of the mind. And we know that actions which are based on such faulty judgments are likely to be disastrous. We are not likely to act well when we are deceived or defrauded.

Some of the most important claims of political theorists, then, turn around the theorist's understanding of what is real—

as opposed to the merely imaginary or the illusory. Many of the most famous political theorists are specifically concerned with dispelling the mists of error which, in their view, becloud men's minds and corrupt their actions. Since rational behavior depends upon an accurate perception of reality, this aspect of a political theory always carries profound prescriptive weight.

To borrow Plato's famous analogy, one important part of the epic political theories is an intent to lead men out from the Cave. In the *Republic*, Plato devotes a great deal of attention to a proposed program of education for precisely this reason. The rigors of the philosophers' education are intended to enable them to distinguish mere appearances from reality. Mere imagining *(eikasia)* is to be replaced by genuine knowledge *(episteme)*. And the political payoff of this reality orientation can be great, Plato believes, for men who have learned to distinguish shadows from reality will be likely to formulate wise political policies.

Most epic political theorists view their task in like terms. They see themselves battling the forces of sophistry and illusion which enchain men politically. At crucial points in their arguments, they insist that this is "really real" and that merely illusory. They attack those political attitudes and institutions which they see as based on false consciousness.

For Marx, his science stands over against all kinds of mistakes about reality. Religion for him is not only an illusion, it is an "opiate of the masses." And the proletariat is also afflicted by what he derisively calls "trade-union consciousness"—a profoundly flawed perception of their situation. On the other side of the class line, the bourgeoisie inhabits its own kind of dream world. Partly because of their own self-interest, the bourgeois thinkers were entrapped by the illusory notions of "bourgeois morality" and by the mistaken idea that the capitalist order was "natural" and immutable.

One key intent of Marx's political theory, then, was to dissipate these dreams and myths. Through the "reform of consciousness," he wanted to break the evil spell which enslaved men's spirits by enchanting their minds. Where Plato spoke of leading men out of the Cave's shadows, Marx spoke in metaphors of waking from a dream. He wanted to analyze the "mystical consciousness" of the world (which he equates with fantasy) and to show that "the world has long been dreaming of something that it can acquire only if it becomes conscious of it." His goal was to shake a mentally slumbering world, to "wake it from its dream about itself," and to make it look at reality for a change.[17]

The whole notion of "the Enlightenment" embodies the same kind of idea. "Enlightenment" was contrasted with the "darkness" of superstition, ignorance, and prejudice. The "Dark Ages" were the historical "Cave," from which reason and philosophy had shown the way out. And the ultimate political outcome would be liberating. Men had been deliberately misled and duped by kings and divines who had a vested interest in controlling them. But the power of reason and science was breaking this spell. Man would be freed, as Kant put it, from his "self-incurred tutelage," and his political deliverance would come from his newly acquired capacity to distinguish what was "really real" from the superstitions and prejudices which had been forced upon him by his rulers.

Machiavelli and Hobbes provide us with our final examples of the prescriptive political force of reality-judgments in political theory, though there are many more of this type.

Machiavelli, one could say, turned Plato on his head—that is, regarding his view of what was real as opposed to what was merely imaginary. Plato passionately argued that true reality was found in "the heavens," in the realm of the Ideas. Men fell into political disasters, he held, by mistaking the "shadows" of this world for ultimate reality. But Machiavelli saw things the other way around. Plato's "realities" were his illusions. In pursuit of "imagined republics" like Plato's, men had brought about their own ruin. The first rule in avoiding these disasters, then, was: Be "realistic." Don't mistake these pretty dreams about what *might* be for an account of the true reality of things. "It appears to me more proper," Machiavelli wrote, "to go to the real truth of the matter than to its imagination; and many have imagined republics and principalities which have never been seen or known to exist in reality; for how we live is so far removed from how we ought to live, that he who abandons what is done for what ought to be done, will rather learn to bring about his own ruin than his preservation."[18]

Hobbes, with his gift of rhetoric, gave us some of political theory's liveliest metaphors of men entrapped by illusions. In his analysis, many of Europe's political afflictions came from two sources: Aristotelian philosophy and the Catholic Church. Both exerted vast power over the minds and actions of men. But both, he contended, were based on fantastic illusions. The "vain philosophy" of Aristotelian scholasticism was "nothing else for the most part, but insignificant trains of strange and barbarous words."[19] And many of the crucial doctrines on which the Catholic Church based its power, he believed, were likewise illusory.

So he depicted the philosophy of Aristotle as a rather dangerous scarecrow and the pope as a ghost. The purpose of his work was to rescue men from domination by these mirages. Concerning the former, he wrote that his theory "is to this purpose, that men may no longer suffer themselves to be abused, by them, that by this doctrine of separated essences, built on the vain philosophy of Aristotle, would fright them from obeying the laws of their country, with empty names; as men fright birds from the corn with an empty doublet, a hat, and a crooked stick."[20] And concerning the Catholic Church, he wrote that "their whole hierarchy, or kingdom of darkness, may be compared not unfitly to the kingdom of fairies; that is, to the old wives fables in England, concerning ghosts and spirits, and the feats they play in the night. And . . . the papacy, is no other, than the ghost of the deceased Roman Empire, sitting crowned upon the grave thereof."[21]

As this quick survey should make clear, fundamental judgments about what is real and what is misleading appearance play an important part in the great theories of politics. And it should also be clear that these claims carry important prescriptive overtones. Shadows, dreams, and fairies do not compel the same response from men as do realities.

It also should be evident, even from this limited sample, that one man's reality may be another man's illusion. But these differences are not simply differences of taste, desire, or preference. They are profound differences of belief about the nature of man and the world. The great political theorists are all reasonable men; but the depth and complexity of their inquiry makes it the kind of enterprise in which reasonable men may differ.

This quality of political theory is what makes its study so fascinating in one way and so frustrating in another. Political theory has the virtue of variety but the vice of indecisiveness. We are each left with the unavoidable responsibility of making our own best judgments on the basis of all the evidence we can find.

"Inconvenient Facts"

Because the complicated judgments about what "is" carry so much prescriptive weight for normal human beings, it sometimes happens that political "ideals" may be undermined by changing "empirical" beliefs. This is what Max Weber, the great German sociologist, had in mind when he spoke about "inconvenient facts" for different political persuasions. By a cumulative accretion of "inconvenient facts," a "normative" political theory may change its shape or even lose its force altogether. No one consciously, perhaps, intended to change or amend the theory. But one day someone begins to realize that the theory has lost its force or meaning through the steady erosion of some of the complex factual premises which sustained it.

An excellent and important example of this pattern is the fate of the classical theory of democracy in recent decades. Several discoveries (or contentions) were made during this period which threatened to cut traditional democratic ideals loose from their factual moorings. First came the claim by the sociologist Robert Michels that the development of ruling elites was inevitable in any society. This contention is his so-called iron law of oligarchy. Next, studies of voting behavior by social scientists demonstrated how far the actual behavior of voters deviated from the democratic norm. The voters were found to be, on the whole, nothing like the "rational" citizenry on which democracy was allegedly based. They did not know how candidates stood on the issues; they did not understand the issues themselves; and they seemed not too concerned to overcome their ignorance. Instead, they were content to vote as their parents had voted, or because they just habitually were attached to a certain party label. And finally, survey data seemed clearly to indicate that these politically ignorant and apathetic nonelites were not very devoted to some of the central democratic "rules of the game"—such as free speech and universal suffrage.

These findings led some students of democracy to suggest a need to revise the classical theory of democracy in order to ground it more solidly in the realities of actual political patterns. At the conclusion of an important study of voting behavior in the 1950s, the authors raised this issue. "How can our analysis be reconciled with the classical theory of liberal political democracy? Is the theory 'wrong'? Must it be discarded in favor of empirical political sociology? Must its ethical or normative content be dismissed as incompatible with the nature of modern man or of mass society? That is not our view. Rather, it seems to us that the modern political theory of democracy stands in need of revision and not replacement by empirical sociology."[22]

Now one can easily argue that these analysts are simply mistaken in their claim that their findings suggest a "need of revision" in democratic theory. Such a revision is at least not logically necessary, in the strict sense. No one can be forced by pure logic to relinquish a particular ideal on the basis of empirical findings about reality. But empirical findings may very well leave an ideal—an "ought"—hanging in midair. Unless he can refute the factual claims, an adherent of the ideal may be left clinging to an ought that is utterly ungrounded in the needs, possibilities, and tendencies of the real world. And the fact is that genuinely compelling ideals do not function this way. When they are completely denied sustenance by facts which support their claim to be realistic, ideals wither and die. They cross the line between meaningful ideal and delusive dream.

That is what these students of voting behavior saw happening to classical democratic theory. If elites were inevitable, it was not realistic to insist upon a wholly egalitarian norm for democracy. Moreover, if, as these findings suggested, the irrationality and apathy of democracy's average citizen was very strong, and disproportionate elite influence seemed to exist, there might actually be a benefit in this apparent inequality of influence, since elite groups were more knowledgeable of and more devoted to the ideals of a liberal democracy. The combination of elite influence and mass apathy might therefore be important in maintaining a stable democratic system. Of course, the classical definition of democracy had to be revised somewhat so that, even with a lessened insistence on equality and participation, what was preserved could still be called "democracy." But this relaxation of the criteria of democracy seemed eminently reasonable since, given the empirical findings, insisting upon equality and participation would be to insist upon the impossible.

In recent years, this "revisionist" theory of democracy has in turn been subjected to sharp criticism. Indeed, this debate continues to be one of the liveliest areas in political science today. The counterattackers have argued in part that the revisionists have been willing to settle for too little—and in the process have jettisoned some of the ideals that are crucial to democracy. To make this case convincing, these "neoclassicists" have also been compelled to direct some attention to facts as well as to ideals. For they recognize that it is hard to claim that the revisionists have settled for too little if they have jettisoned only impossible ideals.[23]

Accordingly, they argue that the so-called iron law of oligarchy isn't really made of iron; that while there may be a strong tendency for all societies to produce oligarchic elites, these tendencies can be minimized and counteracted. The average citizen, they maintain, is neither so irrational nor so antidemocratic as early studies alleged. And they assert that widespread participation in politics, though it may not be necessary to the stability of democracy, is not detrimental to democratic stability—and is important to the individual's own fulfillment as a human being. These empirical claims do not suggest that democratic government in the classical sense is as wholly desirable or as inevitable as some of its early enthusiasts believed. But they do permit the classical democratic ideal the status of a realistic possibility.

Strategies and Trade-offs

The prescriptive recommendations which grow out of a political theory's comprehensive vision of politics are not by any means exhaustive in scope. Generally speaking, the understanding of politics embodied in a political theory eliminates a range of conceivable political actions by making them seem clearly "irrational." This is the exclusionary, "negative" prescriptive function of political theories. Positively, a political theory will suggest what kinds of political arrangements might be conducive to human fulfillment and will indicate what desirable political arrangements might be possible or even necessary. Within the boundaries of these suggestions, many other decisions have to be made before specific political policies or strategies are implemented. The advisability of these concrete and specific actions will depend upon a variety of strategic considerations. Therefore, for example, Marxist theorists and partisans all embrace the goal of the classless communist society but often dispute heatedly over the best means to that end.

The prescriptive dimension of a political theory cannot decide what trade-offs should be made when equally legitimate needs or goods conflict. We live in a world where there often is not enough to go around—where tragic choices often have to be made. Sometimes the only solution to a political problem is a compromise that fully satisfies no one. Sometimes desirable goals may run at cross-purposes. The requirements of political efficiency often collide with steps toward equality, for example, and political stability may require actions that frustrate civil liberty. Political theories, whatever their prescriptive utility, cannot solve these intractable dilemmas which lie at the root of many political issues.

Even here, though, a political theory shapes the way the trade-off is seen. Different theories may indicate different choices in cases such as these because of the judgments about reality, possibility, and necessity which they contain. For example, it is clear that James Madison would put a higher value on freedom than would either Plato or B. F. Skinner. The latter two seem to place a higher value on political stability and unity. But the fact is that the issue looks very different to them—and the choices they make are profoundly shaped by these differences of understanding. They do not all see things the same way and then choose differently. They see the situation so differently that, in a real sense, they don't face the same choice.

For Madison believed that well-devised political institutions can permit great personal freedom within the context of a stable and relatively just political order. Plato, on the other hand, believed that freedom will tend to undermine—and eventually destroy—the unity and integrity of a political society. The two thinkers chose differently—made a different trade-off—in large part because they disagreed about what is possible. (And the jury is still out on this question. Recent years have seen enough liberal democracies succumb to the internal conflicts and stress which freedom produces to lend weight to Plato's assessment. But, on the other hand, Madison's own handiwork, the American constitutional system, has managed to survive for two hundred years.)

B. F. Skinner would make a different trade-off than would Madison where personal freedom and social order collide. But for him it's not really a trade-off at all. "Freedom," he argues, is merely an illusion in any case. All our behavior is controlled and determined by socialization or enculturation, so we might as well be controlled in a way that makes for a unified and happy society. The "trade-off" is only apparent, in his view. Madison and Skinner thus make different choices because they differ in an important way about what is real.

Prescriptions as Counsels of Prudence

The prescriptions of political theory, then, are very much like the prescriptions which we carry to our local druggist. They are like "doctor's orders of a peculiarly compelling kind."[24] They are not so much absolute and categorical moral injunctions ("You absolutely ought to do this, period") as they are sound recommendations for those who value their health ("Take this if you want to get well"). They are counsels of prudence

The great political theorists offer us their counsel, based upon their visions of political reality. And if we come to share their vision, we will be inclined to follow their advice, even "nature itself compelling us." For, as they would insist, they are not merely ventilating their preferences. They are telling us what they think we should do for our own good.

NOTES

[1] David Hume, *A Treatise of Human Nature*, Book 3, Part 1, Section 1.
[2] Theodore Roszak, *The Making of a Counter-Culture* (Garden City, N.Y.: Doubleday, 1969), pp. 79-80.
[3] Thomas Hobbes, *English Works*, vol. I, p. 8.
[4] Ibid., vol. II, p. xvii.
[5] Plato, *Republic*, viii, 566.
[6] Aristotle, *Politics*, 1263a.
[7] Ibid., 1263b.
[8] Edmund Burke, *Reflections on the Revolution in France*, pp. 55-56.
[9] Ibid., pp. 68-69.
[10] Hobbes, *Leviathan*, p. 280.
[11] Burke, *Reflections on the Revolution in France*, p. 38.
[12] Ibid., p. 217. Therefore, Burke goes on to predict, if a monarchical type regime were reestablished in France, it would probably be "the most completely arbitrary power that has appeared on earth." The ascendancy of Napoleon made Burke look like a pretty good prophet.
[13] Madison, *The Federalist Papers*, #47.
[14] Hobbes, *Leviathan*, p. 104.
[15] Aristotle, *Politics*, I, 2, 14.
[16] Rousseau, *Social Contract*, p. 9.
[17] Karl Marx, "For a Ruthless Criticism of Everything Existing," in Robert C. Tucker, ed., *The Marx-Engels Reader* (New York: Norton, 1972), p. 10.
[18] Machiavelli, *The Prince*, chapter 15.
[19] Hobbes, *Leviathan*, p. 604.
[20] Ibid., p. 594.
[21] Ibid., p. 614.
[22] Bernard Berelson, Paul Lazarsfeld, and William McPhee, *Voting* (Chicago: University of Chicago Press, 1954), p. 322.
[23] As Charles Taylor might put it, these defenders of the classical norms of equality and participation recognize that the "value-slope" of the revisionists' underlying empirical theory is too steep for them. So they have to change that by amending some parts of the empirical theory. Taylor's article, "Neutrality in Political Science," is an excellent source for further exploration of the way that empirical findings shape and constrain normative models of politics. The article is contained in *Philosophy, Politics, and*

Society, edited by Peter Laslett and W. G. Runciman, 3rd series (New York: Barnes and Noble, 1967), pp. 25-57.

24 This is J. W. N. Watkins's characterization of Hobbes's laws of nature. J. W. N. Watkins, *Hobbes's System of Ideas* (London: Hutchinson University Library, 1965), p. 76.

SIX

CONCLUSION: VISION, THERAPY, AND THE MASTER SCIENCE

The purpose of this book has been to provide a framework for understanding political theory.

The focus of our account has been principally on the process of inquiry undertaken by the political theorist. We have tried to recreate the living thought patterns of the theorist's mind as he moves from his original puzzlement and concern to his conclusions. We have tried to disentangle and identify the major stages in this process—stages which sometimes are partly latent or all jumbled together in the final product which the theorist leaves to posterity. And we have tried to indicate how each stage sets the agenda for the one which follows it.

Theoretical Investigation

By focusing on the process of inquiry, on the living movement of the theorist's mind, we have been led to a dynamic model of political theorizing. The framework offered here resembles a moving picture more than a snapshot. Like a movie, our account of the enterprise of political theory has a plot and movement. It has a beginning problem and a climax. And, in between the motivating impetus and the denouement, there is the drama and suspense of some very tricky detective work.

The thought process of the working political theorist, in fact, resembles rather closely the investigations of a master sleuth. The theorist's problem, like the detective's, is a break-down of order, although this lapse of order, in the theorist's case, is not an individual crime. Instead it is some kind of disruption within society as a whole.

Beginning with the breakdown of order, the theorist, like the detective, has to look for his "clues." He has to develop his hunches, looking for the deeper nature of the problem he experiences and for the often submerged sources of the prob-lem. Why did this society break down? Why are the lives of its members disturbed and unsatisfactory? Why, in Plato's case, did Athens condemn and execute its noblest citizen? Why, in Hobbes's case, was England so afflicted with social turmoil? Why, in Marx's case, was the mass of mankind so alienated and exploited? Following the theorist's mind as he probes and sifts through the evidence he gathers can be as fascinating as following Sherlock Holmes's battle of wits with his arch villain, Dr. Moriarty.

Finally, the theorist builds his case. He locates what he believes to be the underlying causes that led to the disorder. For example, Hobbes analyzes the body politic into its constituent motions, finds the problem to lie in the dynamics of the human passions, and concludes that it is ultimately the behavior of the power-hungry ego that leads to civil war and, therefore, re-quires containment and control by the state. Or Marx follows his trail of clues back to the institution of private property. Or Burke traces the "ferocity" and "madness" of the French Revolu-tion back to the utopian dreams of France's bourgeois intelli-gentsia.

As these examples suggest, moreover, the theorist is here "building his case" in another sense as well, for his analysis will usually implicate some important people in the "crime." Thus, Plato's examination of the forces behind the death of Socrates results in a *de facto* indictment of Athenian society and its corrupt leaders. Thus, Marx's analysis leads to an indictment of the bourgeoisie—as indicated by the way his moral fury keeps breaking through the veneer of his "scientific" dispassion. Thus, Machiavelli's exploration of the sorry condition of the Italian city-states constitutes an indictment of the weak and timid leaders of those cities. And thus, Hobbes and the Enlightenment liberals, in their very different ways, indict the Catholic Church and the Aristotelian philosophers.

Like the findings of our master sleuth, then, the findings of a political theorist are never really neutral. The theorist tries to be thoroughly "objective" in the sense that he is talking about the genuine sources and the plausible rational responses to very real problems. But his diagnosis will almost inevitably help to legitimate one general course of action as prudent and to disqualify others as unsound.

That is why political theories are controversial; there are very real interests and very high stakes involved. The committed partisan of democracy, for example, will not be inclined to accept Plato's view of the dangerous unreliability of popular opinion or to accept Michels' depiction of the "iron law" of oligarchy without putting up a pretty stiff fight. For conceding the truth of these views would clearly suggest the need for an agonizing reassessment of his political commitments. By the same token, a good Marxist is virtually bound to dissent from Freud's account of human motivation; and a corporate executive can hardly rest comfortable with Marx's analysis of alienation in a capitalist society.

The ideas generated in a political theory have consequences. And those who fear the consequences have a built-in motivation to challenge the ideas. Arguments in political theory are frequently bitter and passionate, because the issues involved are by no means strictly academic. If a given theory achieves widespread acceptance, some men stand to be winners and others losers. Some will be vindicated and others discredited.

The Model

One virtue of our "moving picture" model of the process of political theorizing is that it helps to place the perennial questions of political theory in context. Some very fundamental questions do crop up again and again whenever and wherever men seek to comprehend, in a profound way, the nature of their political predicament. What are the natural desires of men? How can society be ordered to avoid its disintegration into civil war? How can liberty and stability be reconciled, if indeed they can be? How much can we expect politics to contribute to human happiness? By understanding the dynamics of political theory we can understand where and why questions like these arise. And we can understand where they lead—why the answers are important.

Another virtue of our "moving picture" model is that it helps to emphasize the profoundly human quality of political inquiry. Political theories are made from existential situations rather than from abstract "observations." They are produced by men who are deeply and passionately involved in their subject matter. Literally so, in fact—for the theorist, as a member and partial product of the political order he examines, is "object" as well as "subject." His analysis is always in part a self-analysis, and thus political theory is in a sense confessional; for in stating his theory of politics the theorist is also stating his own identity. He is affirming the meaning of his own existence as a political animal.

The force of human passion, after all, is both the alpha and the omega of a political theory. The natural human passion of dismay and distress at being caught up in a traumatic political crisis provides the beginning impetus for the inquiry. And it is the natural human desire to pursue a course of action which is both realistic and calculated to alleviate the distress that gives a political theory its prescriptive force. Delete this side of a political theory, and you are left with the mere husk of a discipline—without force, meaning, or significance. A political theory is a product of what Aristotle called man's "practical reason." It is a body of ideas and perceptions of politics which grow out of the practical task of coping with political problems. The creation of a political theory does not move so much from premise to conclusion as from problem to solution. Its internal dynamic comes not from the compulsion of abstract logic, but rather from the impulsion of thoughtful men dealing with the human political condition.

I have tried to interpret and to illustrate the process of this practical reason in the preceding chapters. The framework offered here has, I hope, several uses for someone who wants to understand political theorizing.

First, our framework should aid in the understanding of an individual political theorist—a Plato or a Rousseau or a Hobbes. The attentive reader should now be able to comprehend the motives and the goals of a political theorist without excessive difficulty. Especially, he should be able to make much more sense of the "logic" of the theorist's inquiry—to perceive the various components of his thought process and to comprehend their relationship. He should be capable of seeing not only what the theorist said but why he said it. And if something seems to be missing or latent in a particular theory—if it seems incomplete—he should be able to identify the missing part and know what to look for.

Understanding the dynamics of political theorizing in this way should also facilitate the comparison of different political theorists. Because they speak from different traditions and from within different social settings, no two political theorists are directly comparable in a simple one-to-one fashion. But the history of political theory is a dialogue, the great political theorists speaking with and to each other. And if the predicaments they face are never identical, they overlap enough to make it meaningful to speak of "common problems" faced by them all. Faced with these similar problems, different political theorists often reach significantly divergent conclusions, so that it does make sense to distinguish between a "Hobbesian" and a "Rousseauian" perspective on politics, for example. The attentive reader should now be able to identify these key areas of disagreement and to see the reasons and arguments behind them.

Finally, the attentive reader may be helped in coming to terms with his own political views. He should be able to dredge up his own "tacit ideology" and see what it looks like. He should be able to identify some of the crucial political beliefs which shape his own political identity and his own political actions. He should be able to locate the underlying judgments which lie behind these beliefs and to subject them to critical scrutiny. In the tradition of Socrates's "gadfly," understanding political theory may sting into consciousness some of the reader's ideas that had been too comfortably taken for granted.

Our framework is only that, of course—although we have tried to fill it in by offering examples from important political theories as we went along. But our examples have been, intentionally, rather brief and capsulized. To flesh out the skeletal structure, the next logical step is to confront the original sources—the classic works of political theory—firsthand. We have tried to illuminate more clearly than political theorists generally do themselves the form and process of political theorizing. For an appreciation of the substance of political theory, though, there is no substitute for direct encounter.

Direct encounter with the classics of political thought should also give life to some of the crucial defining features of political theory touched upon in our analysis. It should become manifest, in the first place, why political theory has often been referred to as the "master science." It should become clear why we have characterized a political theory as a kind of "vision" of politics. And it should also begin to be apparent why political theory has been said to be a kind of "therapy."

The Master Science

Political theory does not warrant the name master science because it is somehow more inherently worthy than other sciences. And it is rather clearly not called the master science because of its greater precision or certitude. Indeed, as we have seen, no political theory can really claim to be certain or provable; there are always some gray areas where guesswork and judgment are required. Instead, the claim of political theory to the title of master science rests upon its unparalleled scope and its unmatched relevance. Political theory is both broader in its reach than any other form of inquiry, and it has a more profound and direct bearing on human action.

A political theory, as a comprehensive vision of politics, incorporates and rests on top of all the other sciences, as the top layer of an intellectual pyramid. The lower levels of the pyramid of most importance for political theory are the particular social sciences, such as economics or psychology; but at times even the natural sciences may become relevant.

Political theory can be said to be "superior" to the other sciences in this specific functional way—just as the top of a pyramid is "superior" to, or above, the bottom layers. The other side of this superior status, however, is a corollary dependency upon the particular sciences underneath. Like the gymnast standing on top of a human pyramid, political theory has to hope that all the members of the pyramid below are reliable. For if any of the "subordinate" layers which support the theory is faulty, the whole structure may fall.

Some political theories rely heavily upon crucial economic doctrines. Marx is, of course, the obvious example here, having devoted volumes to an analysis of the dynamics of a capitalist economy. And the connection between laissez-faire liberalism and classical economics is also very intimate. In either case, the persuasiveness of the political theory depends in large part upon acceptance of the underlying economic models which sustain it.

Even more frequently, psychological theories serve as the foundation for political theories, since it is hard to offer a comprehensive view of politics apart from claims about human nature. Plato's analysis of the different types of society rests explicitly on his account of the different types of human psyche. Hobbes, Rousseau, and Aristotle all offer in their different ways very detailed analyses of the human passions. The political outlooks of Marcuse and Fromm diverge from Freud's pessimism because of their divergent interpretations of the dynamics of the libido. And so on. Almost all political theories incorporate and depend upon psychological analyses of this sort.

Different philosophies of history and theories about human knowledge may also be important underpinnings for a political theory. Both Hegel and Machiavelli, for example, clearly believed that the distinctive virtue of their political theories rested upon their insights into the dynamics of history. Plato and the French *philosophes* devoted a great deal of careful attention to epistemology—the theory of knowledge—because their views in this area seemed clearly pregnant with vast political implications.

Political theorists may even delve into the natural sciences for some of their theoretical building blocks. Hobbes, for instance, devoted a tremendous amount of time to considering the physics of motion, for he believed that the dynamics of "bodies politique" could not be understood unless one also understood the dynamics of "bodies" in general. Similarly, the "social Darwinists" carried the theory of evolution into their analysis of political life. For them, an understanding of politics depended upon a proper understanding of the biological forces at work there.

It is hard to predict, then, what intellectual hallways the reader may enter when he picks up a work of political theory. He may find himself exploring theories of aesthetics or epistemology, biology or economics. But by understanding the way in which the master science is pyramided on top of the particular sciences, he should be able to understand that he is not being subjected to a random intellectual smorgasbord. The political theorist is simply laying the necessary foundations for what is to follow.

Not only should the reader not be distracted by the apparent intellectual detours he encounters in political theory, but he should try to understand why the theorist has chosen his particular route. He should try to see why it is that the theorist considers certain ideas about psychology, or history, or physics so important. For grasping the relationship between the theorist's final political views and the particular sciences on which he builds is one of the real keys to understanding his vision of the world.

Therapeutic Vision and Practical Wisdom

We find ourselves returning once again to that word—"vision"—which has been a recurrent theme throughout our discussion. In closing, then, it is perhaps appropriate to reemphasize one last time that the many metaphors of sight found in political theory are not there by accident. For, as our framework has suggested, a political theory is only secondarily and derivatively a set of abstract "propositions." More concretely and fundamentally, it is an existential sequence of systematically related perceptual judgments.

In its final form, a political theory amounts to a way of seeing. And, since the viewer is himself a part of the politics which he sees, and not merely a detached spectator, the way of seeing becomes a mode of being. Different visions of politics generate different patterns of political action.

After dissecting a political theory to look at its components—its perceptions of disorder, its diagnoses, its reconstruction, and its prescriptions—the final need is to "indwell" the whole vision, to see *through* the eyes of the theorist, rather than simply looking *at* his ideas. It is essential to understanding a political theory to appreciate its logic, to recognize the different stages of the theorist's inquiry and to perceive how each stage relates to the others. But once that task is done, one must move from an analysis of ideas to an imaginative participation in the theorist's way of seeing and experiencing the world.

It is the hope of the political theorist, of course, that this act of sympathetic imagination on the part of his reader will not be purely an academic exercise. His hope is that you will in fact begin to "see things his way"—the way which he is convinced is the right way. A political theorist writes not simply to inform his readers, but also to convert them. He wants to raise, to extend, or to correct the vision of his audience so that they will be enabled to conduct their political affairs more wisely.

The knowledge offered by a political theorist, in short, has therapeutic intent. *Periagoge* (the Greek for "conversion"— literally an intellectual "turning around") leads to *therapeia* (i.e., therapy). The fruit of enlightened vision is practical wisdom, *phronesis*, a kind of "saving knowledge." The wise and knowing man, who sees political things for what they are, knows how to behave well. He knows how to devote his actions toward the establishment of a good and just society.

A political theorist who does not wholly convince you may still change your life by improving your vision. Even if you don't completely see things his way, looking at the world of politics through his eyes may enable you to become attuned to previously unseen realities. It is a poor reader indeed who does not emerge from a confrontation with Plato, or Marx, or

Hobbes, or Rousseau with a deepened awareness of the problems and the possibilities of political life.

When someone asks what the purpose of political theory is, what good it does for those who take the time and effort to study it, I often recall a New Year's card which Adlai Stevenson sent to friends and well-wishers several years ago. "As we enter the new year," he wrote (and I have to paraphrase from memory), "I want to share with you this prayer of an Indian chieftain." In that prayer, the Great Spirit was asked to send his light to shine on "the dark and rocky path along which we goeth leaping."

A political theory is not a gift of divine grace—though it may sometimes strike either its creator or its reader with the force of a virtual revelation. Instead, it is a work of human intellect, produced through arduous effort and often through even more arduous experience. But the plea of the Indian leader cited appreciatively by Mr. Stevenson was for what political theory seeks to provide: some badly needed illumination to help us as we move down that "dark and rocky path along which we goeth leaping."

BIBLIOGRAPHY

Some of the leading textbooks in political theory are listed below.

Ebenstein, William. *Great Political Thinkers: Plato to the Present.* 4th ed. New York: Holt, Rinehart & Winston, 1969.

Hallowell, John. *Main Currents in Modern Political Thought.* New York: Holt, Rinehart & Winston, 1950.

Plamenatz, John. *Man and Society.* 2 vols. New York: McGraw-Hill, 1963.

Sabine, George. *A History of Political Theory.* 4th ed. Revised by Thomas L. Thorson. New York: Holt, Rinehart & Winston, 1973.

Sibley, Mulford Q. *Political Ideas and Ideologies: A History of Political Thought.* New York: Harper and Row, 1970.

Strauss, Leo, and Joseph Cropsey, eds. *History of Political Philosophy.* 2nd ed. Skokie, Ill.: Rand McNally, 1972.

Wolin, Sheldon. *Politics and Vision.* Boston: Little, Brown, 1960.

Some especially useful sources on the nature of political theory include the following.

Berlin, Isaiah. "Does Political Theory Still Exist?" In *Philosophy, Politics, and Society,* 2d series, edited by Peter Laslett and W. G. Runciman. Oxford: Blackwell, 1962.

Bluhm, William T. *Theories of the Political System.* Englewood Cliffs, N.J.: Prentice-Hall, 1965.

Brecht, Arnold. *Political Theory.* Princeton: Princeton University Press, 1959.

Catlin, George. "Political Theory: What is It?" *Political Science Quarterly* 72,1: 1-29.

Cobban, Alfred. "The Decline of Political Theory." *Political Science Quarterly* 67,3: 321-337.

Easton, David. *The Political System.* 2nd ed. New York: Knopf, 1971. (especially Chapter 10)

Frohock, Fred. *Normative Political Inquiry.* Englewood Cliffs, N.J.: Prentice-Hall, 1974.

Germino, Dante. "The Revival of Political Theory " *Journal of Politics* 25,3: 437-460.

Gewirth, Alan. *Political Philosophy.* New York: Macmillan, 1965. (especially the Introduction)

Gould, James A., and Vincent V. Thursby, eds. *Contemporary Political Thought: Issues in Scope, Value, and Direction.* New York: Holt, Rinehart & Winston, 1969.

Hacker, Andrew. *Political Theory.* New York: Macmillan, 1961. (especially Chapter 1)

Kateb, George. *Political Theory: Its Nature and Uses.* New York: St. Martin, 1968.

Macdonald, Margaret. "The Language of Political Theory." In *Logic and Language*, 1st series, edited by Antony Flew. Oxford: Blackwell, 1951.

Partridge, P. H. "Politics, Philosophy, Ideology." *Political Studies* 9,3: 217-235.

Plamenatz, John. "The Use of Political Theory." *Political Studies* 8,1: 37-47.

Runciman, W. G. *Social Science and Political Theory.* Cambridge: Cambridge University Press, 1963.

Sabine, George. "What is a Political Theory?" *Journal of Politics* 1,1: 1-16.

Strauss, Leo. "What is Political Philosophy?" In *What is Political Philosophy?* Glencoe, Illinois: Free Press, 1959.

Taylor, Charles. "Neutrality in Political Science." In *Philosophy, Politics and Society*, 3rd series, edited by Peter Laslett and W. G. Runciman. New York: Barnes & Noble, 1967. (pp. 25-57)

Tinder, Glenn. *Political Thinking: The Perennial Questions.* 2nd ed. Boston: Little, Brown, 1974.

Voegelin, Eric. *The New Science of Politics.* Chicago: University of Chicago Press, 1952.

Wolin, Sheldon. 'Paradigms and Political Theories." In *Politics and Experience*, edited by Preston King and B. C. Parekh. London: Cambridge University Press, 1968. (pp. 125-152)

———. "Political Theory as a Vocation." *American Political Science Review* 63,4: 1062-1082.

Other works cited are listed below.

Aristotle. *Ethics.* Translated by J. A. K. Thomson. Baltimore: Penguin Books, 1955.

———. *Physics.* Translated by R. P. Hardie and R. K. Gaye. In *Great Books Series.* vol. 8. Chicago: University of Chicago Press, 1952.

———. *Politics.* Translated by Ernest Barker. London: Oxford University Press, 1958.

Banfield, Edward. *The Unheavenly City.* Boston: Little, Brown, 1968.

Berelson, Bernard, Paul Lazarsfeld, and William McPhee. *Voting.* Chicago: University of Chicago Press, 1954.

Berger, Peter, and Richard J. Neuhaus. *Movement and Revolution*. New York: Doubleday, 1970.

Berman, Marshall. *The Politics of Authenticity*. New York: Atheneum, 1970.

Boorstin, Daniel. *The Genius of American Politics*. Chicago: University of Chicago Press, 1953.

Burke, Edmund. *Reflections on the Revolution in France*. New York: Liberal Arts Press, 1955.

Cahn, Edmond. *The Sense of Injustice*. Bloomington, Indiana: Indiana University Press, 1949.

Collingwood, R. G. *The New Leviathan*. Oxford: Clarendon, 1942.

Freud, Sigmund. *Civilization and Its Discontents*. Translated by James Strachey. New York: Norton, 1962.

Fromm, Erich. *The Sane Society*. Greenwich, Connecticut: Fawcett, 1967.

Hartz, Louis. *The Liberal Tradition in America*. New York: Harcourt, 1955.

Hobbes, Thomas. *Behemoth*. New York: Burt Franklin, 1963.

————. *English Works*. Edited by William Molesworth. London: John Bohn, 1839.

————. *Leviathan*. New York: Dutton, 1950.

Hume, David. *A Treatise of Human Nature*. New York: McKay, 1898.

Kaplan, Abraham. *The Conduct of Inquiry*. San Francisco: Chandler, 1964.

Kuhn, Thomas S. *The Structure of Scientific Revolutions*. 2nd ed. Chicago: University of Chicago Press, 1970.

Lane, Robert E. *Political Ideology*. New York: Free Press, 1962.

Langer, Susanne K. *Philosophy in a New Key*. New York: Mentor Books, 1951.

Lerner, Michael P. *The New Socialist Revolution*. New York: Delta Books, 1973.

Lifton, Robert Jay. *Revolutionary Immortality*. New York: Vintage Books, 1968.

Lippmann, Walter. *The Public Philosophy*. New York: Mentor Books, 1956.

Lorenz, Konrad. *On Aggression*. Translated by Marjorie Kerr Wilson. New York: Harcourt, 1966.

Madison, James, et al. *The Federalist Papers*. New York: Mentor Books, 1961.

Manuel, Frank, ed. *Utopias and Utopian Thought*. Boston: Houghton Mifflin, 1966.

Marcuse, Herbert. *Eros and Civilization*. New York: Vintage Books, 1955.

———. *One-Dimensional Man*. Boston: Beacon, 1964.

Oakeshott, Michael. "Introduction" to Thomas Hobbes's *Leviathan*. Oxford: Blackwell, 1947.

———. *Rationalism in Politics*. New York: Basic Books, 1962.

Paine, Thomas. *The Rights of Man*. Garden City, New York: Doubleday, 1973.

Plato. *Apology*. Translated by F.J. Church and rev. by Robert D. Cumming. Indianapolis: Bobbs-Merrill, 1958.

———. *Laws*. Translated by A. E. Taylor. London: Dent, 1954.

———. *Republic*. Translated by Francis M. Cornford. London: Oxford University Press, 1945.

Polanyi, Michael. *The Tacit Dimension*. Garden City, New York: Doubleday, 1966.

Roszak, Theodore. *The Making of a Counter-Culture*. Garden City. New York: Anchor Books, 1969.

Rousseau, Jean-Jacques. *The Social Contract and Discourses*. Translated by G. D. H. Cole. New York: Dutton, 1950.

Saint-Simon, Henri de. *Social Organization, The Science of Man, and Other Writings*. Edited and translated by Felix Markham. New York: Harper Torchbooks, 1964.

Sinyavsky, Andrei. *On Socialist Realism*. New York: Pantheon, 1960.

Smith, Lillian. *Killers of the Dream*. Garden City, New York: Doubleday, 1963.

Stillman, Edmund, and William Pfaff. *The Politics of Hysteria*. New York: Harper & Row, 1964.

Strauss, Leo. *Persecution and the Art of Writing*. Glencoe, Illinois: Free Press, 1952.

Toulmin, Stephen. *Human Understanding*. vol. 1. Princeton: Princeton University Press, 1972.

Tucker, Robert C., ed. *The Marx-Engels Reader*. New York: Norton, 1972.

———. *Philosophy and Myth in Karl Marx*. Cambridge: Cambridge University Press, 1964.

Watkins, J. W. N. *Hobbes's System of Ideas*. London: Hutchinson, 1965.

Willhoite, Fred H., Jr. "Ethology and the Tradition of Political Thought." *Journal of Politics*, 33,3: 615-641.

INDEX

INDEX

Burke, Edmund, 13, 20, 30, 40, 67, 106
  on constraint, 115
  and crisis of civility, 36-37
  on French Revolution, 36-37, 114-116, 131
  on organic society, 107
  and Paine, 56-57
  on stability and political theory, 20, 21

Cahn, Edmond, 27-28
Canute, 54
capitalism, and Marx, 37-39, 107
Carroll, Lewis, 103
Castro, Fidel, 22
Catholic Church, 132
  Hobbes on, 122
Christianity, 108
church and state, Locke on separation of, 112
civility, and Burke, 36-37
Civilization and Its Discontents (Freud), 60
civil science, 84
classics, reading, 12-15
classless society, 108, 126
  and aggression, 61
  Freud on, 110-111
  Marx on, 110-111
Cold War, causes of, 74
commodity fetishism, 5
communism, 96-98
  Freud and, 110-111
Communist Manifesto (Marx), 99
community
  morality in, 94-95
  Rousseau on, 94-95
Condorcet, Marquis de, 35
Confessions (Rousseau), 29
conservative, political theory of, 54-55, 56, 87-88

constitution, Aristotle on, 5
constraint
  Burke on, 115
  Hobbes on, 115
  need for, 112-118
conversion, 7
cosmion, 3
crisis
  of *ancien régime,* 35-36
  of Athenian justice, 40-44
  of authority, 31-33
  of capitalism, 37-39
  of civility, 36-37
  of legitimacy, 33-34
  of moral equality, 39-40
  of stability, 30-31
Cromwell, Oliver, 32
Cuba, socialization in, 22

daimon, 42
Dark Ages, 121
decision-making, in society, 2
Delphic oracle, 41
democracy
  revisionist theory of, 125
  theory of, 123-125
  voting behavior in, 123-124
determinism, see historical determinism
Detroit riots, 73-74
diagnosis, 47
  differences in, 66-69
  and ignorance, 36-37
  optimistic, and aggression, 61-66
  other issues in, 69-71, 73-75
  pessimistic, and aggression, 58-61
diagnostic differences, and ideological perspectives, 66-69
diagnostic issues, 69-71
  in recent political controversy, 73-75

Leviathan (Hobbes), 1, 6, 13, 94, 99
liberalism, laissez-faire, 136
liberal society, free speech in, 25
liberty, and Founding Fathers, 91-93
libido
  Fromm and, 136
  Marcuse and, 136
Lifton, Robert Jay, 85
Lippmann, Walter, 28
Locke, John, 3, 12, 21, 30, 32, 33, 71, 106
  articulation in United States, 20-21
  and crisis of legitimacy, 33-34
  on nature of government, 34
  and separation of church and state, 112
logic-in-use, 15, 16, 78
  vs. reconstructed logic, 10-12
Luther, Martin, 58-59

Machiavelli, Niccolò, 17, 29, 30, 44, 131, 136
  and crisis of stability, 30-31
  experience of, 31
  and Plato, 121
Madison, James
  and freedom, 126-127
  on government, 69
  political theory of, 4, 92-93
  on powers of government, 5
  and separation of powers, 115, 116
Marcuse, Herbert, 7-8, 67, 69, 75, 86
  on Freud, 64, 65-66
  on instinctual gratification, 112
  and libido, 136
  on psychology and political philosophy, 55

on repression, 66
marketing orientation, 49
Marx, Karl, 3, 18, 40, 44, 49, 52, 87, 106, 131, 132, 138
  on alienation of labor, 37, 38
  and British working class, 26
  and classless society, 110-111
  on commodity fetishism, 5
  on communist society, 96, 97
  on contradictions in bourgeoisie, 37-38, 70
  and crisis of capitalism, 37-39
  and dialectical change, 96-97
  and historical determinism, 113-114
  and mankind's sins, 37-38
  and mystical consciousness, 120-121
  political theory of, 4, 61
  on private property, 61, 63
  on religion, 120
  and revolution, 70, 96-98
  on self-estrangement, 38, 51, 52
  and trade-union consciousness, 120
Marxist movements, leadership of, 106
master science, political theory as, 75, 135-137
Medici family, 31
Michels, Robert, 123, 132
Mill, John Stuart, 29
Montesquieu, Baron de, 115
moral equality, and Rousseau, 39-40
morality, in community, 94-95
mystical consciousness, 120-121

natural sciences, and political theory, 137
nature, state of, 71-73
necessity, constraints of, 112-118